THE ANSWER TO THE ATHEIST'S HANDBOOK

RICHARD WURMBRAND

VOMBOOKS
The Voice of the Martyrs

The Answer to the Atheist's Handbook
VOM Books
A division of The Voice of the Martyrs
1815 SE Bison Road
Bartlesville, OK 74006

Interior design and layout by Genesis Group

Cover by Julian Davis Design

Printed in the United States of America

ISBN 978-0-88264-165-2 (pbk.)
ISBN 978-0-88264-215-4 (ebook)
ISBN 978-0-88264-216-1 (audiobook)

Library of Congress Control Number: 2022931196

CONTENTS

1

THE ATHEIST'S HANDBOOK

Wherever people know how to write, they have a holy book.

Atheists, too, have one—it is called *The Atheist's Handbook*. It was first issued in 1961 by Moscow's Academy of Science (the State publishing house for political science). This summary of atheistic creeds is the collective work of a great number of specialists, such as historians Beliaiev and Belinova and philosophers Tchanishev, Elshina, and Emeliah. Its final redactor is university professor S. Kovalev.

This book, which has been reprinted many times, has been translated into many languages and widely distributed in other socialist countries. From the primary grades through college, on radio and television, in films and at atheistic rallies, the ideas contained in this book are propagated. And when an atheist dies, the funeral speech assures his brokenhearted family that the dead are dead forever, that there is no comfort for the bereaved, that those separated now will never more be reunited, that there is no God and no such thing as eternal life.

The primary purpose of the book is to show that there is no God.

We could answer very simply with a question: If there is no God, how is it that sheep exist?

The question was actually raised at an atheistic meeting in Russia. The lecturer had explained that life appeared spontaneously and developed through natural selection, and that in the cruel fight for survival only the animals that were stronger or quicker than their neighbors survived, while the weaker succumbed.

A believer asked, "But how is it that sheep survived, that they were not utterly destroyed by wolves? The female wolf produces five or six offspring a year, the sheep only one. The ratio is 5:1 for the destroyer, which has sharp teeth, claws, strength, and swiftness in running. The sheep has absolutely no defense. How is it that there still are sheep? Today man protects them. The animal world existed before man appeared. Who protected the sheep at that time? You can explain many things without resorting to the hypothesis that God exists. But sheep with four legs could not exist without Him, any more than Christ's loving sheep, who have been defenseless against cruel persecutors since the beginning of the Church."

The answer this believer got was a few years in Soviet prisons.

An atheist could get a very simple answer also on the subject of Christ.

At a party of intellectuals, Shakespeare was being discussed. Someone quoted Lady Macbeth's words after she had murdered King Duncan in his sleep. Looking at her bloodstained hands, she exclaims, "Out, damned spot! Out, I say."

A Christian asked the question, "What are the possibilities of a Lady Macbeth being cleansed of her burden of guilt?" One atheist answered, "Man is a reasonable being. A proper education and good advice even at the last minute would have kept her from her ugly deed." The reply was of no help. Lady Macbeth had committed a murder, and philosophizing about the education she should have had was useless. Another said, "I believe that murderers should get the death penalty." This proposal, too, was useless, because a man sentenced to death still dies with the consciousness of guilt. A third man assured those present that in the future happy Socialist society there would be no kings, no selfish ambitions to be gratified, no need or desire to commit crimes. But the fairy tale society exists nowhere.

The believer then said, "The solution of the Bible remains the only valid one: The blood of Jesus Christ cleanses us from all sins."

But we cannot stop with such simple answers. Members of an Academy of Science have written over six hundred pages to prove that religion in general, and Christianity in particular, is false. Let us try to understand them and to answer all the points they raise. It is a duty of courtesy and love to accept the challenge.

The Atheist's Handbook is boring. In fact, it could not be otherwise. Nobody can be eloquent for atheism. Atheism is a denial. Who can write enthusiastically about a negation? Who can address a sonnet to a negation, or dedicate a concerto to a negation, or sculpture a negation? Religion has inspired symphonies, paintings, statues, poetry. Atheism, by its very nature, could never have this impact. Atheism has no wings.

According to its own doctrine, men are only dust and shadow—mere matter. What impetus has matter to destroy religion? Can matter enlist passion in the fight for an ideal when ideals, not being matter, are by definition nothing?

The Atheist's Handbook also uses deceptive methods and a violence of speech which does not suit an Academy of Science well.

We propose to avoid as much as possible the tedium of pseudo-scientific arguments. We will respond, even in the face of irony and slander, with the sweetness of love.

We can afford to take this attitude because good anvils do not fear the blows of many hammers. In Paris there is monument to the Huguenots showing an anvil and a number of broken hammers, with the inscription, "Hammer away, ye hostile bands. Your hammers break; God's anvil stands."

We can take this attitude because we ourselves sift our thoughts with severity and consider it an advantage to be criticized. It is to the detriment of atheism in Communist countries that it imposes a dictatorship. How can one who doesn't bear criticism know he is right?

In all the Christian countries of the West, atheism has full liberty for its propaganda. Christianity has not the slightest reason to fear it. In free debate, only Christianity can win. Imagine two rooms separated from each other by a thick curtain. In the one darkness reigns, the other is lighted by a candle. If the curtain is withdrawn, it is not darkness that prevails. Darkness cannot overcome the light from the candle, because it is not energy. It is the absence of light.

Only light, being energy, can prevail. Thus, the room that was in darkness becomes visible, transformed by the burning candle.

Christians have not feared prisons nor the implements of torture. Neither do we fear atheist books. In the struggle of ideas, the final victory can only be ours.

2

THE REASONABLENESS
OF ATHEISM

Atheists should know, first of all, that we Christians are not their enemies but their friends. We love atheists. And love understands.

We are not surprised that there are atheists.

In the twentieth century, when millions of innocent men, women, and children have been burned in furnaces, gassed, or otherwise killed in concentration camps of different political regimes (some of which proclaimed themselves Christian), it is difficult to believe in a God who is both almighty and good. If He is almighty, why did He not prevent the atrocities? If He is good, why did He create a world of such cruelty?

We cannot reproach someone for being an atheist when high prelates of the Christian church are often on the side of oppressors and exploiters, when they flatter tyrants or fight together with rebels, among whom are those who dream of becoming the tyrants of tomorrow.

When Jesus hung powerless on a cross and cried, "My God, my God, why have you forsaken me?" (Matthew 27:46), it must have been difficult to convince anyone that this crucified Man was the hope of humanity or that the One who thirsted after water but received only vinegar, possessed all power in heaven and earth. It took a resurrection to make the proclamation of the truth possible.

Those who call themselves after the name of the Son of God have killed each other in two world wars. A man baptized in the name of Christ gave the order to drop the first atomic bomb.

And then, even if prodigal sons would like to return to the Father's house, they would not know where to find it. In its stead are many divergent denominations, each claiming to have the truth. They are united in only one point: not to practice the all-embracing love for innocents still behind bars or who have died in concentration camps.

Furthermore, in the minds of multitudes, religion is tied up with superstition, backwardness, or strange dogmas.

Atheism is the effect of these as well as many other causes. We could not expect otherwise; it is only logical that many should be atheists.

God allowed room for atheism in the world. The Bible teaches that God created a material world with intrinsic laws and an endless chain of causes and effects. He allows men to exist. Therefore, the possibility of atheism was contained in the plan of creation, and when it was decided that Christ would atone by His blood for the sins of mankind, He agreed to atone for the sins of atheists, too.

If God allows atheism to exist, who are we to forbid it?

We have full understanding for atheists.

But atheists, on the other hand, have to account for what is from their standpoint an anomaly: Many of those who suffer horribly in this world created by God love Him with all of their heart. Tradition and custom can account for churchgoing and attendance at religious rituals. But how can atheists explain that a burning love for God is sometimes seen precisely in the men who suffer most? How can they explain what Christians call "joy in the Lord," felt by men who are beaten and tortured for their faith and who may have fifty-pound chains at their feet?

Religion is flourishing in some very poor countries. Hungry men gather on Sundays with starving children and sing of the glory of God. Why? How is it that widows with only "two mites" for their living gladly give their last coins in order that God may be served with greater pomp?

The questions posed to Christians by atheists are reasonable. If God is almighty, why does He allow death to rule on earth? Why have I been bereft of my most beloved, asks the atheist? Why does my child suffer or my friend die young?

But how can atheists explain the fact that other men, similarly bereaved or themselves facing death, accept tragedy with serenity and even joy? For them death means to go to the Father.

From the time of building the pyramids, when slaves died under the whip and denial of God or rebellion against Him would have seemed normal, a poem has come down to us:

Death is in my sight today
Like the recovery of a sick man,
Like going out into the open after a confinement.

Death is in my sight today
Like the odor of myrrh,
Like sitting under an awning on a breezy day.

Death is in my sight today
Like the odor of lotus blossoms,
Like sitting on the banks of drunkenness.

Death is in my sight today
Like the passing away of rain,
Like the return of men to their houses from an
expedition.

Death is in my sight today
Like the clearing of the sky,
Like a man fowling thereby for what he knew not.

Death is in my sight today
Like the longing of a man to see his house again,
After he has spent many years held in captivity.

Some men accepted death with serenity, others with joy, considering that to die meant to return to the world of the spirit.

Some plants are heliotropic, turning toward the sun. But there are also plants which grow only in shade or darkness, just as there are men who love God in proportion to their suffering for Him. These are the ascetics, the martyrs. They lovingly bear all the hardships about which the atheists complain. Suffering does not make them swerve in their faith; on the contrary, some are brought to faith or strengthened by deep suffering.

Oscar Wilde cared nothing for God and led a life of depravity. In the end, this genius found himself in jail under the most degrading accusations. Under these circumstances, he wrote, "If the world has been built of sorrow, it has been built by the hands of love, because in no other way could the soul of man for whom the world was made, reach the full stature of its perfection."

In Dostoevsky's *Crime and Punishment*, Raskolnikov has a discussion with Sonya, a prostitute. She took this profession because her father was a drunkard and her younger brothers and sisters hungered. She suffered terribly under this condition imposed upon her by bitter circumstances. Raskolnikov asked her, "You pray to God a lot, Sonya?" She answered in a whisper, "What would I be without God?" He, probing deeper, asked again, "But what does God do for you in return?" Her reply is, "Don't ask me. You don't deserve to know...He does everything."

Raskolnikov also questioned her poor, miserable, younger sister Polenka: "Do you know how to say your prayers?" Her answer was, "Oh, of course, we all know; we have for ages. Now that I am a big girl, I say my prayers to myself, but Kolya and Lida say them aloud with Mama. First they say, 'God, bless and forgive our sister Sonya,' and then, 'God, bless and forgive our second father,' because our first daddy is already dead, and this one is our second one."

How is it that the Sonyas and Polenkas love God? Could their religion be only a pain reliever like drugs or alcohol? But drugs and alcohol destroy the minds of men. Her faith in God made Sonya so strong that she could bring to repentance the murderer Raskolnikov and lead him to become a new man. So there must be some kind of reality behind her faith.

Sonya gave to Raskolnikov a cross and read to him from the Gospels. This made an undiscovered murderer surrender himself to the police, go to Siberia, and start a new life. What would have happened if she had given him the hammer and sickle and had read to him one of Stalin's tedious speeches or Marx's *Das Kapital*?

Sonya, caught in the tragedy of prostitution, and Raskolnikov, awakened from the tragedy of crime, believed.

For many, religion is just one of the many joys of life, a refinement like art or luxury. But there are those to whom it means everything, who pant after God as the deer pants after rivers of water. These claim to know God. They say that He is lovable and trustworthy, even if His ways are mysterious and if life is very hard on them.

They understand the atheist phenomenon. But can atheists understand them?

In September 1932, a Moscow magazine, *Molodaia Guardia* (*The Young Vanguard*), announced that in accordance with the atheistic five-year plan, by 1937 every manifestation of religion must be definitely destroyed and the Word of God must be silenced forever. But this did not happen. On the contrary, Christianity was flourishing, even in Communist countries, though long prohibited and threatened with persecution. Why?

Atheism is reasonable only when it discovers the reason for deep faith.

3

THE UNREASONABLENESS OF ATHEISM

Society is changing very quickly. Religious systems have not kept pace with the transformations. Often, preachers comment on debates Jesus had with men two thousand years ago regarding problems of that time, instead of providing answers, in the Spirit of Christ, to the problems of modern man. Therefore, many come to the conclusion that religion is irrelevant.

In addition, many rituals are obsolete.

Further, churches assert their wish to save men from a future hell. Then they should prove their love toward men by helping save the world from today's hell of illiteracy, hunger, misery, tyranny, exploitation, and war.

Christians accept all of this criticism from atheists. "Love... believes all things" (1 Corinthians 13:7). We can believe the reasons for being an atheist. We say with Hegel, "Everything which exists is reasonable." Even an atheist's attitude can have profound reasons. But atheists are at a disadvantage when they refuse the criticism of believers.

The man united with God's Spirit can understand those who do not worship because they know not God. The Christian mind mirrors the whole of reality, the atheist mind only part of it.

Atheists have a materialist philosophy that Christians share. The principal doctrine of our religion is that God has become flesh (i.e., matter) in Jesus Christ. The Christian God is not an idea, but a Person. The aim of Christianity is not only the salvation of souls, but the resurrection of the body in incorruptibility.

But we don't stop at materialism. Materialistic atheists are one-sided: they do not know about the Godhead and the eternal Spirit of love and truth who rules this world.

Has anyone ever seen a coin with only one face? Or electricity with only one pole? Christianity embraces the realm of the spirit as well as the material. Because it is one-sided, atheism is false.

A fool was sent to buy flour and salt. He took a dish in which to carry his purchases. He was told not to mix the two ingredients but to keep them separate. After the shopkeeper had filled the dish with flour, the fool, thinking of the instructions, inverted the dish, asking that salt be poured on the upturned bottom. Therewith, the flour was lost, but he had the salt. He brought it to his boss, who inquired, "But where is the flour?" The fool turned the dish over to find it. So the salt was gone too.

Atheists sometimes act like this man. They bring very earnest and useful criticisms against religion. They have the salt. But do they not thereby lose the flour? Do they not throw away arguments *for* religion which may also be right? And in the end will they not have to shed the salt of atheism, too, in moments of deep crisis? It is the pride of true Christianity to have the flour and the salt. Its philosophy is what Soloviev called "Theomaterialism," comprehending matter and *Theos* (in Greek, God), its creator. Indeed, Christianity is so sure about the truth it possesses that it is open to all criticisms of this truth; yes, it even welcomes such criticism as a spur that ensures a better ride on the horse of truth.

Faith lives by continual rejection of errors and continual acceptance of inspiration from quarters where new truths have been experienced.

Once the sun quarreled with the moon. The sun said, "The leaves on trees are green," whereas the moon said that they are the color of silver. The moon asserted that men on earth generally sleep, whereas the sun said that usually all men are moving.

The moon asked, "Then why is there such a silence on earth?" "Who told you this?" the sun answered. "On earth there is much noise." The strife lasted for a long time.

And then the wind came; he listened to the debate and smiled. "Your quarrel is in vain. I blow when there is sun and when the moon shines. During the day, when the sun shines on the earth, everything happens just as the sun said. There is noise on earth and men work and the leaves are green. By night, when the moon rises, everything is changed. Men sleep, silence reigns, and the color of the leaves changes to silver. Sometimes, when a cloud covers the moon, they even look black. Neither you, sun, nor you, moon, know the whole truth."

Atheists look at the material side of things and believe they encompass all reality. Buddhists believe that mind is the only reality and that the material world belongs to Maya, the sphere of illusion. But the Bible uses, in Hebrew as well as in Greek, the same word for "spirit" as for "wind." It blows at all times, from many quarters. Those who have the Spirit of God see the whole of reality. They cannot limit themselves to either the materialist philosophy or the idealist one.

As a matter of fact, the Bible warns us to be careful in philosophical matters, because most philosophers have individual points of view from which they look at reality. But every point of view is a point of blindness: it incapacitates us for every other point of view. From a certain point of view, the room in which I write has no door. I turn around. Now I see the door, but the room has no window. I look up. From this point of view, the room has no floor. I look down; it has no ceiling. By avoiding particular points of view we are able to have an intuition of the whole. The ideal for a Christian is to become holy, a word which derives from "whole." In Russian the word "holy" (*sviatoi*) suggests luminosity. The same is true in the Germanic idioms. To be holy means to have abandoned points of view.

Feuerbach said, "It is clear as the sun and evident as the day that there is no God; and still more, that there can be no God." It is not religion which asserts absolute clearness, but atheism. If the non-existence of God is as "clear as the sun," how is it that all mankind (without exception) acknowledges the existence of the sun, but not all mankind subscribes to the assertion of Feuerbach that there is no God?

Not even Darwin, the great favorite of my opponents, could adhere to it. He wrote, "The impossibility of conceiving that this grand and wondrous universe with our conscious selves arose through chance, seems to me the chief argument for the existence of God."

For atheists, atheism is self-evident. Then why the need to propagate the obvious? Christians do not consider Christianity as self-evident as the fact that two and two are four. If it were so, there would be no atheists. We find some of the attitudes of our opponents sensible. There is a place in our understanding for them. Atheism has only atheism and denies to religion every right to exist. Therefore, it is not sensible.

Max Stirner, the theoretician of individualist anarchism, rightly saw the evils of society. His solution was to liquidate human society. But he was a part of it. Schopenhauer's school recommended suicide to mankind as the answer to its problems. But when cholera broke out in his town, he fled. He loved life. In the same category are those who wish to get rid of religion itself because of its great shortcomings in thought and deed.

Should we give up wearing coats because some have an unpleasant color? Should we throw away the clean baby with the dirty bath water?

We have acknowledged what is reasonable in atheism. There is much besides. Now let atheists seek together with us what is reasonable in religion. Maybe we will arrive at a common denominator.

4

THE WRONG PERSPECTIVE OF THE ATHEIST'S HANDBOOK

The authors of *The Atheist's Handbook* have written a book about the greatest problems of life, problems over which the greatest minds have pondered since man began: the existence of God, the sense of life, its hopes and sorrows, the role of religion, and so on.

Who are these individuals? It is much more important to know them than the contents of their book.

To know the teacher is much more valuable than to know his teachings. Knowledge always proceeds from "What am I?" If I do not know the answer to this, how do I know that what this "I" thinks is worth being shared with others? If the "I" is not great, everything it gives will be small change.

Atheists say that they were not created by any God. There was no design in the random processes of matter that produced them. Can the whirling of atoms and protons and their accidental coming together produce a brain that will distill pure truth?

I was a poor child. I would have liked to learn music, but my parents could not afford it. So I wrote music notes at random on a lined piece of paper. But they never produced a melody.

If, say, in the game of roulette there are two possibilities that a red or a black number will come up, the chance of a number turning up in the same color forty times in a row is perhaps one in one hundred million. This when there are only two possibilities!

How many chances were there that such a perfect computer as the human mind should be produced by an accidental union of electrons and protons? I, the author of this book, speak many languages and know something like one million words, if I count all the inflections of the verbs and nouns. Like any cultured man, I have millions of bits of knowledge of mathematics, geography, physical science, art, etc., at my command. Yet at any given moment the mind can extract exactly the right word, with exactly the correct intonation, backed by the most suitable attitude expressive of character that the occasion requires. The probability that this one phenomenon—let alone the organization of the whole universe—could be the product of an accidental coming together of elementary particles, arising from nothing, is mathematically impossible.

If I count three generations in a century and begin to calculate how many ancestors I have—two parents, four grandparents, eight great-grandparents, and so on—I quickly reach figures of tens of millions of men from whom I have inherited a genetic stock. I am the selected product of a struggle for life in which millions of predecessors were involved. What do I know about them? Nothing.

What do I know about the heredity I have received from them? They formed the language in which I think, they created the institutions in which I was brought up. I do not know them. I do not know my own childhood, which is the most decisive period in the shaping of a future teacher of atheism or religion.

I live in an unspeakably small world. Our earth is a bit of dust in the universe. We consider it a noteworthy achievement to have reached a minuscule satellite of this speck of dust. On our small earth, the biosphere is a small thing; so also mankind that dwells in the biosphere. As for me, I am a most insignificant individual among billions.

Scarcely one in ten thousand will have ever heard the titles of the greatest books that have been written. Not one in a million will have read them. How many know about the existence of a most reverend bishop or about a member of the Soviet Academy, co-author of *The Atheist's Handbook*?

I once had a lapse of memory. I could not remember who had written *Crime and Punishment*. It was only the twentieth man I asked who could tell me that it was Dostoevsky.

We are infinitely small, and we know as much about what should rather be called the pluriverse than universe, as an ant knows about Marxism after walking over a book by Marx.

I enjoy the chirping of birds, not knowing which of them will be captured by an eagle this very day. I hear the wind passing through branches, but I do not know which tree is being eaten by a worm. We are greedy for fame, power, money, pleasure, knowledge. Those who had the same greed a couple of decades before us are now clay.

Bukharin was one of the greatest theoreticians of Communist atheism. In his book *Dialectic Materialism*, he began by praising this philosophy because, he said, it allows for the possibility of foreseeing the future. The only thing the poor man did not foresee was that his own comrades would torture and kill him.

It is a daring thing to write a book, to become a teacher of humanity. Can one know what joys and tragedies will be experienced by future readers, and whether one's book will be helpful in moments of great trial?

Does a man know even one of the billions of cells that constitute his brain? A small disturbance in them can make one write foolish things. This has happened to geniuses. Can it happen to you? You recognize madness in the writings of others. Can there be none in yours? You know nothing about your body. What do you know about the depths of your psychology? I am daily a surprise to myself.

We live mysterious lives in a mysterious world, of which we know only some fringes. We are imprisoned in the jail of our senses.

If there were on earth beings that could emit rays outside the spectrum of our vision, if they could communicate among themselves on a wavelength beyond those we hear or apprehend, then they could observe us and we would never know anything about their existence, just as we lived for millenniums without knowing about the influence of viruses and microbes on our lives. What if angels do exist and we are unable to perceive them?

Atheists assert that there is no God. How can they be sure?

The book you are reading was conceived in a prison. The guards regularly searched our cells for forbidden objects, such as chessmen, knives, needles, books, and paper. They did not find them. We waited until they had left. Then we took them out of their hiding places. You search a cell for an object and you do not find it. But is it right to maintain that it is not there? Who has searched the infinite universe to ascertain that there is no God?

Therefore, can you know for sure the things which you assert?

Until recently, it was considered a certainty that the simple elements were immutable. This was an assertion based on thousands of years of experience, but nevertheless it was false. Men of considerable intellect were sure that the atom was indivisible and that man could not fly to the moon. These, who had the overwhelming experience of mankind on their side, erred. How many chances have you to be right?

The Christian teacher Tertullian has been much belittled for his words *"Credo quia impossibile est"* (I believe because it is impossible). And now science makes real just what appeared absurd and impossible to reason.

We are small and insignificant. We do not know. "If anyone imagines that he knows something, he does not yet know as he ought to know," says the Bible (1 Corinthians 8:2).

5

WHO ARE OUR OPPONENTS?

If a plainclothes man asks me to show him my identity, my first reaction is to ask him who he is. He has to prove that he is from the police. Otherwise he has no right to question me.

If I confront the incomprehensible reality of the universe and ask the sphinx, "Who are you? Is there a Godhead in you? Were you created by an artist or have you existed from eternity?" I might receive the reply: "Tell me first who you are, little man. Are you of such worth that the ultimate mysteries should be revealed to you? And if I were to share them with you, would you have the capacity to understand and to accept truth in all its purity, even if it were contrary to your own interests and to everything you believed and cherished until now?"

The authors of *The Atheist's Handbook* deny the existence of God. But do they themselves exist? Who are they? Can they prove their own existence?

In order for an atheist author to pose daring questions, he has to posit, billions of years before his birth, the existence of galaxies and astral dust. There had to be stars and celestial mechanics and a sun to regulate the movement of the earth, without which life would have been impossible. The atheist can ask daring questions precisely because there exist water, herbs, animals, and micro-organisms, and such realities as electricity and heat, risen bread and fermented wine, cosmic rays and falling rain, and the over-whelming reality of human personality. There had to be a whole line of ancestors, and milk in his mother's breast, and love in her heart.

Even assuming the atheist's presuppositions, an unfathomable reality has produced—through the interaction of time and chance over an incomprehensible period of billions of years—both an atheistic lecturer and a Christian saint. Why? Who are they? Why are they? In fact, are they?

You know as much about this as you know why the earth, together with the whole solar system, runs uninterruptedly toward a certain constellation, as if it had an appointment. They are attracted. But what is this universal attraction? Attraction is a word which we use sometimes for lovableness. Who loves? Who is the beloved?

Atheists speak, as do preachers. How about leaving their con-fusing voices and listening to the voices of leaves, brooks, winds, storms, birds, little children? These might be more instructive than many of our words.

Those who live in tune with nature believe. Atheism started as an urban phenomenon in the distorted minds of those who had to live behind walls, social as well as structural.

And what about listening to the great silence? From where came the beauty of snowflakes, flowers, ferns, lichens, each a different piece of exquisite embroidery? From where came the wonderful arrangement of elementary particles in the atom?

How is it that the electron revolves in its orbit hundreds of millions of times every hundred-thousandth of a second, so that what is in constant motion should give us solid objects to handle?

Did you ever hear about a machine with eighty trillion electrical cells? One of its parts, weighing only fifty ounces, is a mechanism consisting of ten billion cells, which generate, receive, record, and transmit energy. This wonderful machine is your body. How grateful you would be if somebody presented you with a car. But you were given a much finer machine. By whom?

How is it that chemical changes in the neurons of the brain become, with a change of sentiments, another thought? How is it that a man exhaling the poison carbon dioxide transforms it into a word of love, or even a word carrying the message of eternal life?

How is it that when you wish to do an evil thing, it is as if an unseen hand would restrain you? Whose hand is this? Even if the voice of conscience is not powerful enough to make you abandon a wicked intention, you hear it later in the form of regret and remorse.

Who are you to ask reality's identity? What if this reality should answer, "Since in your arrogance you set yourself up as an authority, please indicate first who you are?" Could you indeed answer one of the thousands of questions that reality asks you? The development of science has not so much increased the knowledge of facts as it has increased the number of questions to which we must find the answers.

You question reality about its last mysteries, about its sense, about its design, about the existence of a Creator. To whom should reality answer, and in what language? Primitive tribes, to which the first missionaries went, had no words for such concepts as "love," "faith," "forgiveness," "spirit," "holy," "train." The missionaries were restricted in their ability to communicate their message or to share the realities of their own country. Have you a common language with the highest reality?

And again, to whom should this reality speak? You acknowledge only reason. But according to your materialistic doctrine, reason is the manner in which the human brain works. The elephant's brain is otherwise constituted. Its work is called instinct. To yours, you have given a nicer name. And yet both brains, you insist, are accidents of evolution, the random agglomeration of atoms over eons of time, without the impinging of a designer.

You consider atheism to be the truth. But before applying the notion "truth" to atheism, you have to define what you mean by "truth."

Pilate asked, "What is truth?" (John 18:38). Whoever does not know the answer to that question has no basis on which to assert that anything is true.

Skeptics have said that "truth is a suspicion that has endured" or "a hallucination agreed upon by a majority." But what they mock as hallucination might be error pointed in the right direction. Alchemy and astrology were just such fruitful errors, precursors of chemistry and astronomy.

What is your definition of truth?

A Marxist would say that truth is conditioned by social class. The economic conditions in which a man lives determine his convictions.

In a letter to Cluss dated December 7, 1852, Marx describes his own economic condition. He says that he is as good as imprisoned because he lacks trousers and shoes and that his family risks being plunged into deep poverty. We are moved to feel sorry for him. But then Marxism is the mentality of men without trousers and shoes. Today, all proletarians in the West have trousers and shoes, more than one pair. So Marxism does not suit us. We have to have a truth of our own.

Marxism proclaims itself as truth and has no valid definition of the word.

It is interesting that Marxism, allegedly the doctrine of the proletariat, excludes proletarian thinkers from truth. Marx writes in a letter to Sorge, dated October 19, 1877: "The workers themselves when . . . they give up work and become professional literary men, always breed 'theoretical' mischief and are always ready to join muddle-heads . . ." The radical student movements also cannot have truth. Marx writes about "the stupid nonsense the Russian students are perpetrating which is worthless in itself." Apparently for Marxists there is only one valid definition of truth: "Truth is what you think when you have no trousers and shoes." For some mysterious reason trousers seem to be a terrible hindrance to the possession of truth. Let us leave all this.

We will serve our opponents with a current definition: Truth is the consistency of the object of thinking (reality) with its product, our own mentality. However, such a consistency is no confirmation that you have apprehended reality rightly. Otherwise, how can you account for the existence of error? You assert that religion is error. But religion is the consistency between reality and another man's mentality. So a man can be very sure about the justice of his manner of thinking and still be mistaken. What if you were the victim of such a delusion?

Suppose a Christian became an atheist. He would then acknowledge his prior thinking to be false. With his mind open to error, he would embrace your ideology. How could he know for sure that he had not fallen into another wrong belief? He might feel sure his thoughts now correspond to reality. But thus he believed when he was still religious. Do you not see that there must be a light beyond reality and pseudo-reality, beyond what we call truth and error, to tell us with authority which is which? Even atheist convictions can exist consistently (how rare is consistency in human thought) only by acknowledging this supreme Light, which we adore in religion.

Should the Highest speak with you in the language of reason? But how much can reason comprehend? Reason justified slavery, absolute monarchy, superstition. It made us cheer dictatorships and justify world wars, which were mass-slaughters of innocent beings. Mephistopheles says of man, "He calls it reason and uses it only to be more animalistic than any animal." Man must always rationalize, conceptualize, and intellectualize all things.

Goethe suggested two centuries ago that "our planet is the mental institution of the universe." We have the reason of a race that has flickerings of genius and truth but shows clearly that it has gone mad. Even with the wisest of us, reason is only a harmony among irrational impulses.

Reason, in order to produce right results, would have to be unsullied by low sentiments and animated by noble desires.

Why should you seek right results if you are not animated by a passion, the love of truth? So a passion, a powerful sentiment, while sometimes a hindrance, can in other instances be a driving force for right reasoning. It is its very presupposition.

How do we know that syllogisms produce right thinking? Well, we just feel it. And we feel it not only in small things, but also in great ones. Einstein said of his famous theory, before it was ever submitted to the crucible of experiment, that he felt it to be true. What is this feeling? It does not belong to reason. Neither does intuition. But they satisfy an Einstein.

Evidence is not only external. There is also inward evidence which sometimes contradicts our senses. This inward conviction, faith, is itself one of the great facts of the universe. It must be respected and explained like any other fact of nature.

The reasoning of Einstein was based on presuppositions outside of reason.

Atheism also rests on a faith. It too has its presuppositions. It rests on the feeling that it is worthwhile to spend life denying the nonexistent. Nietzsche, the great prophet of the anti-Christ, had the honesty to acknowledge this. He wrote: "Even we, devotees of knowledge today, we, godless ones and anti-metaphysicians, still take our fire, too, from a flame, which a faith, thousands of years old, has kindled: that Christian faith, which was also the faith of Plato, that God is truth, that truth is divine." Nietzsche was sorry about it, but he considered himself "still pious."

If sentiments play such a big role in the convictions of believers and unbelievers alike, why should the Highest speak to you, proud reason, and not to these sentiments?

Lenin says in his *Philosophical Copybooks* that matter has the capacity for self-reflection. It reflects itself in thinking. In whose thinking? In that of a person. Now, if whatever we think is a reflection of reality and if all our thoughts are so very personal, the truth which they reflect must be a Person, whom we apprehend clearly or dimly, or in a distorted manner, or even without knowing whom we really apprehend. Jesus said that the Truth is a person—Himself. Just try to express this in a syllogism. You will come to the conclusion that Jesus' assertion must be true, a mysterious truth.

If you do not have the sentiment of mystery, you cannot arrive at the truth.

Why do you believe what your mind tells you? You know that it is unreliable. You just arose from hours of sleep in which this same mind tricked you with an illusory world. It lies to you every night. It lies in your daydreams and in your fancies. Is it reasonable to rely blindly on your mind?

Millions of men, relying on their minds, cheered a Hitler and a Stalin as great geniuses. These same minds later indicted them as mass-murderers. You have often discovered your mind to be in error. It does not even pretend to tell you the truth. It is deceitful and self-serving, telling you rather what you would like to hear. It tells the atheist that there is no God; it tells the religionist that he can be comfortable; it tells the member of any political party that its program is the best.

We have all made great mistakes. The whole history of mankind is a big cemetery of ideas for which men were ready to die. Are you sure that your ideas will not one day be considered as stupid as the idea that the earth is borne by Atlas?

Relying on their minds, ninety-nine percent of men, even of our century, believe in the absolute validity of the law of causality. But Heisenberg is right, along with the very few who understand his assertion: "The resolution of the paradoxes of atomic physics can be accomplished only by renunciation of old and cherished ideas. Most important of these is the idea that natural phenomena obey exact laws—the principle of causality."

Did you ever visit an asylum? Where is the barrier between an asylum and everyday life? It might lie in a microbe of syphilis lodging in the brain of a genius or in an unbearable emotion that caused a brilliant mind to disintegrate. Do the authors of *The Atheist's Handbook* know what spirochete may have begun its destructive work in their brain? Khrushchev described Stalin's regime as a hell in which even Communist leaders had to tremble for their lives. Thus even the authors of *The Atheist's Handbook* must have endured terrible trauma. Can they be sure they are completely sane? Is any one of us? We belong to a race which, while living on a rich earth, finds no other solution to its problems than a general massacre every thirty years. There must be something wrong with our minds. Are atheists justified in relying on their minds?

What man could not be categorized at least in part as a maniac, a neuropath, an addict, a man obsessed, a schizophrenic, a megalomaniac, a pervert, a man with a confused mind? Where is the perfect, normal mind?

Who are you, mind? Show your identity! Who is your ultimate authority, whom you can question about reality and ask to reveal to you its final secrets?

There arises on the surface of the ocean of reality a minuscule drop—my being. It arises within the ocean. It cannot leave the ocean even for one moment. My being is a part of it, ravaged by its tempests.

As soon as my self poses as a king and wishes to judge the reality, instead of humbly feeding on it, I am no more a reality, but a nonentity, an illusion.

There exists only one reality—God. He has created, but within Himself. In Him we have our being, life, and movement. He engulfs all that He creates. Just as billions of cells, every one with a complete organization and having all the functions of life, receive their existence from the body, live by it and in it, so we are all part of a higher reality. We live in God. When we oppose ourselves to Him, our existence loses its meaning.

Wise men know how to take a joke, even if they are its subject. Without malice, we will tell our atheist friends a joke:

The Central Committee of the Communist Party of the Soviet Union discussed the problem of Khrushchev. Brezhnev and others said, "He is an idiot. Let us get rid of him." Podgornyi intervened: "But now it is possible to transplant organs. Let us transplant in him the brain of a genius." The others consented. A surgeon was called and the operation successfully completed. But it did not provide the expected result. They had forgotten about the phenomenon of rejection. The brain of the genius rejected Khrushchev.

Take it as a joke! But an enlightened mind, a mind enlightened by its Creator and in harmony with Him, rejects atheist doctrine.

6

THE DIFFICULTY OF
BEING AN ATHEIST

We have set ourselves to go as far as possible toward an encounter with our atheist friends.

Atheism can be the passage from false religion to spiritual truth. Atheism in one age is generally the result of the superstitions of a hypocritical religion in the preceding one. But then it is a passage. Do not stop in the passage!

We also know that not all who call themselves atheists really are. Baron Holbach, one of the eighteenth century's renowned atheist philosophers, called God his personal enemy. For him, nothing other than nature existed. Nature, according to him, creates everything, being itself uncreated. But this is exactly what we believe about God! Nature is infinite and eternal. Again, this is what we believe about God. In nature, there are laws, order, purpose, spirit. The more you read what Holbach understands by nature, the more you have the impression that he has only substituted the word "nature" for "God," for whom he had an aversion. This is not real atheism.

For many, atheism is only a screen for the frustration of an unsuccessful religious search. Their atheism is repressed religiosity, and it is our fault that we do not know how to communicate with them. Christians should unlearn "Christianese" when they deal with unbelievers. Doctors use an idiom of their own when they are among themselves, but the wise physician, when dealing with a patient, uses a language understood by him. Not all teachers of religion nor all Christians know how to make their faith intelligible to those who are not used to biblical language. This keeps many away from religion.

Therefore, we must have understanding.

We also sympathize with the burdens of an atheist. To be an atheist is surely much more difficult than to be religious. Atheists have a very exacting belief. They reproach us for believing without proof. We will present the proofs of our faith in this book. But who will ever be able to prove the stupendous dogmas of atheism?

Its first dogma is: "From eternity there has existed matter in continual movement, which has created life."

How do atheists know this? The renowned astronomer Hoyle adduces proof to the contrary. In *Nature of the Universe* he writes:

> To avoid the issue of creation it would be necessary for all the material of the universe to be infinitely old. And this cannot be for a practical reason. For if this were so, there could be no hydrogen left in the universe. As I think I demonstrated when I spoke about the insides of the

stars, hydrogen is steadily converted into helium throughout the universe, and this conversion is a one-way process; that is to say, hydrogen cannot be produced in any appreciable quantity through the breakdown of other elements. How is it then that the universe consists almost entirely of hydrogen? If matter were infinitely old, this would be quite impossible. So we see that the universe being what it is, the creation issue simply cannot be dodged.

We also know that according to the second law of thermodynamics, in all observable physical processes in the universe, some energy becomes less available. The universe is running down. Since it is far from run down, it must have had a beginning.

The Bible speaks scientifically when it says, "The things that are seen are transient" (2 Corinthians 4:18).

What proofs do atheists have to the contrary? What makes them believe that matter has existed forever? What proof that it has always been moving? Yet you have to believe it, and believing it is very hard. It is hard to believe that there is no God, no loving Father, no purpose in things, no hope for our life which soon runs out.

Is everything a chance gathering of elementary particles? The Communist writer Anatole France wrote, "Chance is perhaps the pseudonym of God, when he did not wish to sign."

Men are not atheists in times of great crisis or danger, in moments of ecstasy from love or the contemplation of beauty. Rare are the atheists who remain godless on their deathbed. Some, it is true, continue to play their role to the end; they would not confess with their mouths, even in the last moments, the doubts by which they are assailed. But whenever a skilled religious personality is near the deathbed of such a man, he succeeds in bringing him to conversion.

A major crisis in life may also shake an atheist's convictions.

When the Russian Revolution was in greatest danger, as Petersburg was surrounded by the troops of the anti-Communist general Kornilov, Lenin delivered a speech in which he exclaimed several times, *"Dai Boje"*—"May God grant that we escape." It might be objected that this is a common saying in the Russian language. But Lenin never used it except in this moment of deep crisis.

Three men led the war against the Nazis: Churchill, Roosevelt, and Stalin. The first two were Christians. Churchill has written six volumes of memoirs about this war. The name God never appears on the lips of the two believers. It is only Stalin who says, "May God give success to the operation 'Torch' (the invasion of North Africa)"; "The past belongs to God"; and so on.

Mao was a fierce atheist. But in 1936, when as a member of the Central Committee of the Communist Party he fell very sick, he demanded to be baptized and received baptism from the hand of a nun. When his wife was shot by the troops of Chiang Kai-shek, he composed a religious poem, "The Immortals." In an interview with the American newspaperman Snow in 1971, he said, "Soon I will have to appear before God."

Now, such incidents are very instructive. If you are an engineer who has built a bridge, the fact that a cat passes over the bridge is not proof that the bridge is good. A train must pass over it. We cannot consider atheistic doctrine profitable if it is only a fair-weather teaching.

Zinoviev, president of the Communist International, died at the hands of Stalin. His last words were, "Listen, Israel, our God is the only God." Yagoda, Soviet Minister of Interior Affairs, also killed by Stalin, said, "There must be a God, because my sins have reached me." Yaroslavski, who was founder and president of the League of the Godless in the USSR, told Stalin from his deathbed: "Burn all my books! Look, He is here! He waited for me. Burn all my books!"

Sitting in Communist prisons with Communists jailed by their own comrades in Party purges, I have been witness myself to similar scenes.

I would recommend that our atheist friends ponder these things.

7

THE DEFINITION
OF RELIGION

The Atheist's Handbook begins with an analysis of different definitions of the word "religion" given by philosophers.

But neither Plato, who said that religion is right behavior toward the gods, nor Plutarch, for whom religion is midway between atheism and superstition, is mentioned.

The book begins with later thinkers and, sorry to say, with falsehoods. Not one of the quotations is correct.

Carlyle wrote, "A lie should be trampled upon and extinguished wherever found. I am for fumigating the atmosphere, when I suspect that falsehood, like pestilence, breathes around me."

Plato had taught that authors of books should consider themselves as priests. The evil of using falsehood consists not only in the lie that passes for truth, but in the fact that men eventually lose faith in other books.

The story is told of a Bedouin who once traveled on a camel through the desert. A man stopped him saying, "Please, make a place for me on the back of the camel, as I have a long journey." The owner of the camel honored the request, and the stranger mounted behind him. Suddenly, as they rode farther, the stranger with a skillful movement threw the owner from the camel and fled. The owner cried after him, "I am not angry because you have stolen my animal. I have many more camels. But I am sad that you have made it harder for anyone in the future to be helpful to a man he meets on the road."

The Atheist's Handbook cares nothing about truth or trust.

My opponents quoted Immanuel Kant as having written that religion is the understanding by man of moral duty. Following are the words of this philosopher, quoted directly: "Religion is morals in reference to God as legislator. It is the recognition of our duties looked upon as divine commandments."

My opponents say that Ludwig Feuerbach defined religion as the connection between men. This again is false. In his book *The Essence of Christianity*, he says, "Religion is the dream of the human mind."

Even the definitions given by atheist authors are falsified. Salomon Reinach is quoted as having taught that religion is a system of contradictions. We find the correct text in his book *Orpheus:* "Religion is the sum of superstitious beliefs which hinder the legitimate working of man's faculties."

That they found it necessary to falsify the words of William James is understandable. They could not quote his opinion: "A man's religious faith (whatever more special terms of doctrine it may involve) means for me essentially his faith in the existence of an unseen order of some kind in which the riddles of the natural order may be found explained...It is essential that God be conceived as the deepest power in the universe and that, secondly, He must be conceived under the form of a mental personality."

The Atheist's Handbook is unjust also toward James Frazer. As quoted, he also appears to be irreligious, when his real words in his work *The Belief in Immortality* are: "The question whether our conscious personality survives after death has been answered by almost all races of man in the affirmative. At this point, skeptic or agnostic people are nearly, if not wholly, unknown."

Not even mentioned are the definitions of such men as Schleiermacher: "Religion is the feel of absolute dependence upon the unseen determiner of our destiny accompanied by the conscious desire to come into harmonious relations with it"; or Emerson: "Religion is communion with the Oversoul, the divinity within us reaching up to the Divinity above"; or Jacob Burckhardt: "Religions are the expressions of the eternal and indestructible metaphysical craving of human nature. Their grandeur is that they represent the whole supersensual complement of man, all that he cannot himself provide. At the same time, they are the reflections upon a great and different plane of whole peoples and cultural epochs."

The authors of *The Atheist's Handbook* don't even try to get light about the word "religion" from its various etymologies which have been proposed. Cicero derived the word from *relegare*—"to consider." With Augustine it means the finding again of something lost. Lactantius sees in it a derivative of *religare*—"to tie" (to a higher power).

But the most curious thing is that the authors of *The Atheist's Handbook*, while claiming to be Marxists, omit the saying of Karl Marx from the list of various definitions of religion, embarrassed, no doubt, because of the beauty of his definition and because of the compliment which he pays to religion.

Christians at odds with each other about being Orthodox, Catholic, or Protestant would feel reluctant to remind their listeners about the words of Jesus: "A new commandment I give to you, that you love one another: just as I have loved you, you also are to love one another. By this all people will know that you are my disciples, if you have love for one another" (John 13:34,35). So Marxists simply cannot quote Marx in matters of religion, because he wrote in *Observations of a Young Man on the Choice of a Life Work:* "To men God gave a universal aim—to ennoble mankind and oneself." And much later in life, in *Contributions to the Critique of Hegel's Philosophy of Right* he wrote: "Religion is the sigh of the oppressed creature, the heart of a heartless world, just as it is the spirit of a spiritless society."

The importance of these words is increased when you realize what Marx had learned from Hegel. Heinrich Heine tells about the latter: "One beautiful starry evening, we two stood next to each other at a window and talked of the stars with sentimental enthusiasm and called them the abode of the blessed. The master

(Hegel) however grumbled to himself, 'The stars, hum, hum, the stars are only a gleamy leprosy in the sky.'"

To have for a teacher somebody with only this to say about the stars and then to give to religion such beautiful definitions is quite an achievement!

It is true that Marx adds, "Religion is the opiate of the people," but put in the context above, these words lose their anti-religious meaning. Opium soothes pain. There is nothing intrinsically evil in opium. Only the discovery of anesthetics made possible the tremendous development of surgery.

Marx, generally, had a great weakness for religion. It was a favorite topic of his. In his monumental *Das Kapital*, he simply says, "For such a society [he means a society based upon the production of commodities; every society produces them], Christianity with its cultus of abstract man, more especially in its bourgeois development, Protestantism, Deism, etc., is the most fitting form of religion."

Thus, every Protestant Christian can prove his case from Marx. He can tell his "Marxist" opponents that they abuse the name of their teacher. A true disciple of Marx must be Protestant, if he wishes to have a fit religion. To think how many Protestants have been jailed and killed by allegedly Marxist rulers!

Though an atheist, Marx had a bias toward religion. His was a split personality. Only later did the disciples of Marx make of his words "religion is the opiate of the people" a terrible charge against us.

People have used many things besides religion as opiates. One man, in order to escape family grief, chooses chemistry as his opiate. He passes all his time in the laboratory and discovers a useful medicine. Is the value of the medicine diminished because the research for it was an opiate to a distressed heart? If one who has met with great adversities in life takes refuge in the quiet of an astronomical observatory, his work is for him an opiate, but the stars which he observes are real. So religion may be an opiate for many, but the Godhead to whom they appeal can be true.

Atheism and revolutionary activities are often an opiate for children of broken homes, a substitute for rebellion against parental authority. Atheism can be an opiate to soothe one's conscience, which otherwise would give pain for the commission of gross sins. Atheism stifles the reproaches of conscience, just as an opiate alleviates physical pain.

Marx's "religion is the opiate of the people" is something entirely different from Lenin's "religion is a sort of spiritual gin," or the inept conclusions of Bakunin: "If God exists, man is a slave; but man can and should be free; therefore God does not exist." It is like saying, "Atheists claim there is no God. But faith in Him gives me relief. So atheists do not exist."

It would have been nice if the authors of *The Atheist's Handbook*, writing so much about and against the Bible, had mentioned the definition of religion given by an apostle of Christ: "Religion that is pure and undefiled before God the Father is this: to visit orphans and widows in their affliction, and to keep oneself unstained from the world" (James 1:27). Are our opponents really against religion thus defined? I contend that no sensible man can be other than charmed by this definition. Perhaps what our atheist friends are fighting against is not even religion but a falsification parading as such. Who can be against caring for the needy and being unspotted from the great filth of the world?

8

THE ORIGIN
OF RELIGION

"Religion is not inherent to man. It is not an inalienable quality of human nature." Our honored opponents say that science has proved this. "The archaeological discoveries have shown that during hundreds of thousands of years, man did not have any religion."

I am not a member of an Academy of Science. In my ignorance, I have believed that archaeology could discover only things which existed in the past, not things which did not exist.

But there is no joking with academicians. They have a powerful argument. Caves have been discovered in which lived the Pithecanthropus and the Sinanthropus, the ancestors of modern man. There were plenty of stone tools and bones of eaten animals. "But never have excavations from that time shown the least sign of some religious representation, even the most elementary, existing at that time."

This reminds me of a story. An Italian debated with a Jew: "You Jews are so proud. There is tremendous propaganda claiming that you are the most intelligent people in the world. Sheer nonsense! In Italy, excavations have been made, and in some strata of the earth at least 2,000 years old, wire has been found, which proves that our Roman ancestors at that time already had the telegraph." The Jew answered, "In Israel, excavations have been made in parts of the earth 4,000 years old and nothing has been found, which means that we had the wireless before you had the telegraph."

What if the absence of any religious relics in the shelters of the earliest men was an indication that they had a spiritual form of religion without outward signs of cult—a religion consisting of meditation, contemplation, and worship in the truth? Let us be honest, comrades, academicians!

But to continue the argument, my opponents have to explain how it happened that at a certain moment man became religious. They say that religion appeared in the time of Neanderthal man for two reasons. First, primitive man's fear of death, coupled with the fear that deceased members of the tribe would come out of their graves and harm the living. Second, primitive man's impotence in the face of the elements of nature.

Now, Pithecanthropus was more primitive than the Cro-Magnon and Neanderthal. He was more impotent than the latter two. So, logically, he should have been more religious.

I appeal to common sense.

My opponents are academicians, some of them historians. What do they hold about the origin of the Russian people and state? Well, they orient themselves to the oldest written documents of our history.

Then this procedure must hold good also in the sphere of the origin of mankind. The oldest documents of mankind are the Maneva-Dharma-Sostra, the Gilgamesh epic, the Vedas, the Egyptian Book of the Dead, the books of Moses, and so on. They are unanimous in saying that we were created by a heavenly being, who disclosed to prophets of old the essential truths that different religions have in common. This would be the origin of religion.

If I am wrong in accepting the oldest written documents of mankind, authors of *The Atheist's Handbook* are wrong in their history of Russia.

On no continent is there any cuneiform tablet, any inscription carved on tables, or any reminiscence that man originated from the ape. Men usually know something about their grandfathers. If men of old had sufficient fancy to invent a sophisticated religion, why did they not remember seeing their grandfathers swinging from trees by their tails?

Again, let us be serious, academicians! Religion comes from God. It is communion with God.

The most primitive man knows "I exist," and "the many objects around me exist." But if I and my fellow men and the things about us exist, there must exist one more thing: existence itself. If I am and the world is, there is also the simple fact of "being." I get old, fellow men die, warning me that my turn will come, while my children grow up. All objects which surround me decay or wither away. But the simple fact of being never ceases. There exists a pure Being, independent of our coming and going. I have not always existed. The things around me have not always been. Primitive men perhaps could not put this in so many words. But they knew about a supreme, immortal Being, the One whose name will be revealed later as the God whose name is "I AM." Belief in Him and the desire to propitiate Him have inspired every religion in its beginning. This is the basis of every religion even now.

If this is not true, why was your book written?

A Russian farmer was once asked by an atheistic lecturer if he believed in God. He answered affirmatively. He was asked again, "Why should you believe in Him? Did you see Him?" "No," was the reply. "But neither have I ever seen a Japanese. Notwithstanding I believe that Japanese exist. Our army fought against them in the last war. This is proof enough for me. If there were no God, why do you fight against Him?"

Why do atheists write 700 pages against a nonexistent person? *The Atheist's Handbook* also belongs to the category of "being" and presupposes an Eternal Being.

9

THE ORIGIN OF CHRISTIANITY

The Atheist's Handbook begins by complimenting us Christians. It says:

> At least in the initial period of its existence, Christianity not only renounced the offering of sacrifices, but likewise also all kinds of ritual. F. Engels asserted that this was a revolutionary step. Differing from the other religions of antiquity, Christianity refused categorically all ethnic delimitations in matters of faith, its sermons having been addressed to all tribes and peoples. In problems of creed, Christianity has categorically refused also the social barriers. Those who propagated the teaching of Jesus spoke to all men, without difference of ethnic origin and social position.

It is not true that the first Christians renounced the offering of sacrifices. True, they abolished the animal sacrifices. But they gladly sacrificed themselves.

In any case, for once our opponents say good words about us. No national or racial discrimination within Christianity, and this already 2,000 years ago! In Poland and in the Soviet Union, there was discrimination against the Jews. In Russia all the Tatars, the Chechen, the Ingush, the Kalmiks, the Balkar, the Volga-German peoples were deported for no other guilt than belonging to a certain nationality. In Communist China, the Tibetans are oppressed. In these countries, the first question asked was, "What is your social origin?" Woe to you if your father happened to possess a factory. There were no social barriers in Christianity as Christ taught it.

The Atheist's Handbook does not compliment us further.

It asserts, "The Greek, Roman, and Jewish authors of the first century give us absolutely no information about Christianity." Notice the nice word "absolutely." The denial is absolutely false.

10

ROMAN AUTHORS ABOUT CHRISTIANITY

The Roman historian Tacitus lived around the years AD 60–120. Referring to the burning of Rome, which happened in AD 64, he writes:

> All the endeavors of men, all the emperor's largesse and the propitiations of the gods, did not suffice to allay the scandal or banish the belief that the fire had been ordered. And so, to get rid of this rumor, Nero set up as the culprits and punished with the utmost refinement of cruelty a class hated for their abominations, who are commonly called Christians. Christus, from whom their name is derived, was executed at the hands of the procurator Pontius Pilate in the reign of Tiberius. Checked for the moment, this pernicious superstition broke out, not only in Judaea, the source of the evil, but even in Rome,

that receptacle for everything that is sordid and degrading from every quarter of the globe, which there finds a following.

Accordingly, arrest was first made of those who confessed (to being Christians); then, on their evidence, an immense multitude was convicted, not so much on the charge of arson as because of hatred of the human race. Besides being put to death, they were made to serve as objects of amusement; they were clad in the hides of beasts and torn to death by dogs; others were crucified, others set on fire to serve to illuminate the night when daylight failed. Nero had thrown open his grounds for the display and was putting on a show in the circus, where he mingled with the people in the dress of a charioteer or drove about in his chariot. All this gave rise to a feeling of pity, even towards men whose guilt merited the most exemplary punishment; for it was felt that they were being destroyed not for the public good but to gratify the cruelty of an individual. (*Annals* XV, 24)

So the "absolute" of *The Atheist's Handbook* is not absolute. We have one Roman historian of the first century witnessing to the existence of Christ.

We can serve our opponents with a second: Suetonius (c. AD 75–160). He writes in *Vita Claudii* (XXV, 4):

> Since the Jews were continually making disturbances at the instigation of Christus, he (Claudius) expelled them from Rome...

So again the existence of Christ is ascertained, yea more: under the emperor Claudius, this Christ already had a multitude of disciples in Rome. In the year AD 64, they were already fiercely persecuted, as the same author describes in *Vita Neronis* (XVI):

> In his (Nero's) reign many abuses were severely punished and repressed, and as many new laws instituted;...punishment was inflicted on the Christians, a sect of men adhering to a novel and mischievous superstition.

There follows a third Roman historian, Pliny the Younger (c. AD 62–113). He writes to the Emperor Trajan:

> It is my rule, Sire, to refer to you in matters where I am uncertain. For who can better direct my hesitation or instruct my ignorance? I was never present at any trial of Christians; therefore I do not know what are the customary penalties or investigations, and what limits are observed. I

have hesitated a great deal on the question whether there should be any distinction of ages; whether the weak should have the same treatment as the most robust; whether those who recant should be pardoned, or whether a man who has ever been a Christian should gain nothing by ceasing to be such; whether the name itself, even if innocent of crime, should be published, or only the crimes attaching to that name.

Meanwhile, this is the course that I have adopted in the case of those brought before me as Christians. I ask them if they are Christians. If they admit it, I repeat the question a second and a third time, threatening capital punishment; if they persist, I sentence them to death.

We can serve our opponents with a fourth document. We possess the first letter of St. Clement, bishop of Rome, dating from immediately after the Neronian persecution or after that of Domitian. It is from the first century and contains plenty of information about Christianity. From it we know the state of the church in Corinth at that time. It tells us that the apostle Peter died as a martyr, that Paul had been in prison seven times. We get the names of other martyrs, the Danaids and Dircae.

St. Clement, writing in the first century, knows Christ as a historical reality. He writes, "Christ is of those who are humble-minded and not of those who exalt themselves over his flock.

Our Lord Jesus Christ, the scepter of the majesty of God, did not
come in the pomp of pride or arrogance, although he might have
done so, but in a lowly condition, as the Holy Spirit had declared
regarding him."

A passage from Sulpicius Severus, a Christian writer of the
fourth century, has also been critically examined and is judged to
have been based upon an extract from a lost writing of Tacitus. It
tells us about a council of war held by Titus after the capture of
Jerusalem in AD 70. Titus is reported to have expressed the view
that the temple of Jerusalem ought to be destroyed so that the religion of the Jews and of the Christians might be more completely
extirpated. The Christians had arisen from among the Jews, and
when the root was torn up, the stem would easily be destroyed.
(Donald Spence, *Early Christianity and Paganism*, New York: Dut-
ton & Co.)

In AD 125 the Christian philosopher Aristides presented to
the emperor Hadrian a full codex of the moral principles of the
church, which must have been old already in order to have so
elaborate a system of thinking.

I quote from it:

> Those who oppress them [the Christians] they
> exhort [with the Word] and make them their
> friends. They do good to their enemies. Their
> wives, O King, are pure as virgins, and their
> daughters are modest. Their men abstain from
> all unlawful sexual contact and from impurity,

in the hope of recompense that is to come in another world.

As for their bondmen and bondwomen, and their children, if there are any, they persuade them to become Christians; and when they have done so, they call them brethren without distinction.

They refuse to worship strange gods; and they go their way in all humility and cheerfulness. Falsehood is not found among them. They love one another; the widow's needs are not ignored, and they rescue the orphan from the person who does him violence. He who has gives to him who has not, ungrudgingly and without boasting. When the Christians find a stranger, they bring him to their homes and rejoice over him. When a baby is born to one of them, they praise God. If it dies in infancy, they thank God the more, as for one who has passed through the world without sins. But if one of them died in his iniquity or in his sins, they grieve bitterly and sorrow as over one who is about to meet his doom.

Such, O King, is the commandment given to the Christians, and such is their conduct. As men who know God, they ask from him requests which are proper for him to give and for them to receive; and because they acknowledge the goodness of God towards them, lo! on their account there flows forth the beauty that is in the world. The good which they do, they do not shout in the ears of the multitude, that people may notice; but they conceal their giving as a man conceals a treasure. They strive to be righteous as those who expect to behold the face of their Messiah and to receive from him the promises.

Truly this people is a new people, and there is something divine mingled in the midst of them. Take their writings and read them; you will find that I have not put forth these things on my own authority. The things I have read in their writings I firmly believe, not only about the present but about things to come. There is no doubt in my mind that the earth stands today by reason of the intercession of Christians. Their teaching is the gateway of light.

Let those approach, then, who do not know God, and let them receive incorruptible words which are from all time and eternity, that they may escape from the dread judgment which through Jesus the Messiah is to come upon the whole human race.

What has remained of the assertion that the first century gives us absolutely no information about Christianity?

But I did not need to argue that it is not true that there are absolutely no documents about Christianity dating from the first century. The academicians, authors of *The Atheist's Handbook*, contradict themselves on succeeding pages. They say that the Book of Revelation is dated AD 68. So we are in the first century. A Jew wrote it. And he begins by telling about an already existing and organized Christianity, even in places far away from Palestine. The Revelation begins with seven letters to the churches of Asia Minor.

11

THE WITNESS OF
THE GOSPELS

That the Gospels were not written in the first century is an axiom for *The Atheist's Handbook*. They were supposedly written by late, clever forgers. The Gospel of John was allegedly written only at the end of the second century.

But Ignatius quoted from it, although he was martyred before the year 116. Justin the philosopher quoted it. He died around 140. Even Loisy, the French critic of the Bible, admits that this Gospel was already received in Rome by the year 130.

A simple analysis of the contents of the Gospels shows that they could not be late forgeries. (In asserting this, my opponents put themselves in opposition even to Engels, who ridicules the idea that Christianity is the work of deceivers. See F. Engels, *Bruno Bauer and Ancient Christianity*.)

At the end of the second century, when the Gospels were allegedly invented, the names of the apostles were highly respected in Christian circles. Why then should a forger, who wished his writing to be accredited as God-inspired, tell the churches that

Jesus called Peter "Satan" and also rebuked the other apostles? Such words would never have appeared in the Gospel if they had not really been said. The apostles were highly esteemed in the church. Deprecatory words about them would not have been invented by Christians.

At the end of the second century, Christ was worshiped as God in the whole church. Every forger foolish enough to attribute to Him a narrow friendship with women or a weakness that made Him cry on the cross, "My God, my God, why have you forsaken me?" (Matthew 27:46) would never have had this book accepted as a holy book. The same applies to the description of Jesus' fear and anxiety in Gethsemane. Such incidents made the name of the Savior open to attack.

Celsus, in a book dated AD 178, mocks Jesus because of His anguish on the cross, reminding us that His disciples endured suffering in brave silence. He must have known the facts about Jesus from the Gospels. The evangelists did not write them down to accomplish their own self-serving purposes but simply because they had witnessed them; and they did not care if the sighs and tears, suffering and pain would degrade Jesus in the opinion of many. Such accounts are the proof of the genuineness and early age of the Gospels.

Late forgeries would have been full of adulation for Jesus. They would not tell us that He was considered by some of His contemporaries, by His own people, as a devil (Mark 3:21,22).

The Gospels and the Epistles retain some Aramaic words. Aramaic was the language spoken by the Jews in Palestine. If the Gospels were written at the end of the second century in the

Greek-speaking world, why would the forgers have retained the Aramaic utterances? They made sense only in the first decades of Christian history, when the majority of Christians were Jews.

The Gospels contain big debates between Jesus and his adversaries about the right manner of keeping the Sabbath and about the value of Jewish ceremonies. For Jewish readers of the first century, these were important. Gentile Christians of the second century would not have understood or been concerned with what the discussions were about. A forger would have had to explain the meaning of phylacteries, a tithe, the Jewish ablutions, who the Pharisees and Sadducees were, etc. But the authors of the Gospels take this knowledge for granted, because they wrote very early and recorded the episodes of the life of Jesus exactly as they happened.

Nowhere in the New Testament do we find the slightest trace of a church in a village. Christianity must have been primarily an urban phenomenon. Why then should forgers have put in the mouth of Jesus continual allusions to country life, to birds and flowers and farming?

We have known in this century masters in forgery. They painted the nimbus of a deity around a man whom they themselves afterwards denounced as a criminal. Forgers must be clever men. If the Gospel writers had been forgers, they would not have made such terrible mistakes, nor would they have succeeded in having their books accepted as sacred Scriptures.

A detail of the Gospel narrative which proves its historical accuracy, as well as its old age, is found in John 19:34. We are told that when one of the soldiers pierced the side of our crucified Lord with a spear, "at once there came out blood and water." The reason is not given. But the Evangelist John had been an eyewitness, and he wrote what he had seen. Neither he nor anybody else at that time could explain what happened. Only after eighteen centuries did a Doctor Simpson, discoverer of chloroform, show that Jesus Christ died from what is called in scientific language extravasation of the blood, or in modern language, a broken heart. When one dies in this way, the arms are thrown out (of course, Jesus' arms were already stretched out on the cross); there is a loud cry, such as Jesus uttered; and "the blood escapes into the pericardium and prevents the heart from beating. There the blood stands for a short time; it separates into serum (the water) and clots (the red corpuscles in the blood). When the soldier pierced the back (pericardium), the blood and water flowed out."

Is it conceivable that a writer would have made up an account of facts which never occurred, but for which a strictly scientific explanation, fitting precisely the facts, could be given only after nearly two thousand years?

The story about the Gospel being a late forgery is in itself a late forgery.

Is it conceivable that a nonexistent, mythical personality was the Creator of the whole Christian civilization, the citizens of which outnumber those of any earthly empire?

No empire has existed for two thousand years, as has the Christian empire, which has survived the persecution, hate, and privations of twenty centuries.

Christianity is the greatest fact in the world—and this greatest fact was produced by a nonexistent personality? Sheer nonsense! Who can believe such a thing?

John Stuart Mill wrote: "It is no use to say that Christ, as exhibited in the Gospels, is not historical. Who among His disciples, or among their proselytes, was capable of inventing the sayings ascribed to Jesus or imagining the life and character revealed in the Gospels? Certainly not the fishermen of Galilee and certainly not St. Paul."

Who could have invented the personality of Jesus—not only His goodness and meekness, but His genius in dealing with people and problems, His insight and ability as an evangelist?

And then who would be the inventors of Jesus? Jews could not have invented Him, because in the first century their monotheism was so stubbornly maintained that they would never have invented a man as representing the incarnation of their unseen God.

Jews despised other nations. They would not drink a cup of water from the hands of a Samaritan, so they certainly could not have invented Jesus, who made friends with foreigners. They believed in themselves as the chosen race: why should they have invented someone who obliterated all race distinctions and embraced all men?

Nor could the first Christians have invented Him.

We see from the beginning that far from being able to invent a Jesus, they could only spoil His beautiful name.

Paul already writes that in his time the majority of those who preached did so out of greed, covetousness, a desire for fame, and selfish motives, and had distorted the word of God. Greedy and selfish preachers cannot invent a Jesus.

And even if men had succeeded in inventing an incarnate God, they would never have invented Him as a Jew, a man belonging to a despised race, and a carpenter at that, a man without learning, who was born in a manger and died on a cross and who has not left one written sentence behind Him.

Such things could not be invented.

Three questions were spoken by the devil when he tempted Jesus in the wilderness: "If you are the Son of God, command these stones to become loaves of bread"; "If you are the Son of God, throw yourself down [from the pinnacle of the temple], for it is written, 'He will command his angels concerning you,' and, 'On their hands they will bear you up, lest you strike your foot against a stone'"; and "All these [all the kingdoms of the world and their glory] I will give you, if you will fall down and worship me" (Matthew 4:3–9). Referring to the three questions, Dostoevsky writes in *The Brothers Karamazov*:

> If there has ever been on earth a real, stupen-
> dous miracle, it took place on the day of the
> three temptations. The statement of these three
> questions was itself the miracle. If it were pos-
> sible to imagine simply for the sake of argument
> that those three questions of the dread spirit had
> perished utterly from the books and that we had
> to restore them and to invent them anew and
> to do so had gathered together all the wise men
> of the earth—rulers, chief priests, learned men,
> philosophers, poets—and had set them the task
> to invent three questions, such as would not only

fit the occasion, but express in three words, three human phrases, the whole future history of the world and of humanity—dost thou believe that all the wisdom of the earth united could have invented anything in depth and force equal to the three questions which were actually put to thee thence by the wise and mighty spirit in the wilderness? From those questions alone, from the miracle of their testament, we can see that we have here to do not with fleeting human intelligence, but with the absolute and eternal.

Ingersoll, a well-known atheistic writer, said about Jesus:

With Renan, I believe Christ was the one perfect man. "Do unto others what you would that they should do unto you" is the perfection of religion and morality. It is the summum bonum. It was loftier than the teachings of Socrates, Plato, Mohammed, Moses, or Confucius. It superseded the commandments that Moses claimed to have gotten from God, for with Christ's "do unto others" there could be no murder, lying, covetousness, or war.

The perfect man could not be invented by very imperfect apostles.

12

ARGUMENTS AGAINST THE EARLY ORIGIN OF THE GOSPELS

But let us not be unfair. We have brought so many arguments of our own as to forget the weighty arguments of the academicians against the early origin of the Gospels. There are three:

1) The Gospels report the expelling of merchants from the temple. "But there has been no commerce in that temple." How the doctors in atheism know this, they do not say. But we will quote from the Talmud, which is surely an accepted reference on Jewish affairs and a higher authority in this matter than my opponents. In the treatise Shabbat, it says that forty years before the destruction of the temple, which means just within the lifetime of Jesus, there were shops in it.

2) "The Bible writes about a herd of 2,000 pigs in the district of the Gadarenes in Palestine. But the breeding of pigs has been forbidden to the Jews from the time of the Old Testament. Therefore, in Palestine there could not exist herds of pigs."

What opinion do you, dear reader, have about the conclusiveness of this argument? Be respectful! Academicians are speaking. There can be no criminality in our country because the law forbids it. There cannot be any quarrel between Chinese, Russian, and Yugoslavian Communists because proletarian Internationalism forbids it. Do these propositions sound plausible?

Besides, Moscow's Academy must have a geographical section, which should know that Gadara was in Peraea, east of the Jordan, a region which properly did not belong to Palestine and was not populated by Jews only.

3) The authors of the Gospels could not be Jews because they do not mention animals native to Palestine at that time, such as wildcats, jackals, and panthers.

Another very convincing argument!

By the same token I might be led to believe that *The Atheist's Handbook* was not written in the Soviet Union because lice, bugs, and rats are not mentioned in it. But I know how much Christians suffered because of these in prison, in the earliest years of terror.

I have done justice to my opponents. I have considered their arguments about the Gospels, too, not just mine. It is for the reader to judge their comparative value.

13

THE MESSAGE OF THE NEW TESTAMENT

The criticisms brought against the New Testament as being a phantasmagoric, late forgery are unfounded.

But if so, why were they brought?

Suppose that the New Testament was a bad book; why then are 700 pages written to refute it? Every year in the Soviet Union there used to appear good and bad—sometimes very bad—novels. Nobody leads a worldwide crusade lasting decades against a bad novel. Readers themselves discard it. The line of the Communist Party in the USSR kept changing. Books considered great were suddenly banned. Years ago who would have dared to have a library without the great genius Stalin's books? But one day an order came. The books simply disappeared. Nobody refutes them. They are buried in silence, as if they had not been written. Then Khrushchev began to publish his more modest collection of articles and speeches, well edited, so as not to remind the reader that he had been one of Stalin's flatterers. These books also disappeared. No refutations. Nobody refutes the tens of volumes of Trotsky.

Why is it that fights are led to criticize, to tear to pieces the New Testament, while at the same time the Soviet population was forbidden to have a copy of it, from which they might have been able to form their own opinion?

Beliefs must rest upon evidence open to examination. What science implies is not so much the importance of any particular truth as the right to seek truth and extend its usefulness unhampered by restrictions. Particular beliefs can survive only so long as they justify themselves against opposition.

Then why have people in Communist countries been prevented from having the New Testament?

It is because the Gospels and the New Testament as a whole contain a message of paramount importance for every man.

Can anyone imagine a good dinner without a cook? But nature is a banquet. There are in nature wheat and potatoes and milk and meat and fruits of many kinds. There are sunshine and rain, lovely flowers and the joyful chirping of birds. There are things useful and things beautiful, to satisfy your body and gladden your soul. Who is the cook at the banquet of nature? It is a wise Creator, God.

It is said that a scientist, coming home from his laboratory, was called to supper by his wife. A salad was set before him. Being an atheist, he said, "If leaves of lettuce, grains of salt, drops of vinegar and oil, and slices of eggs had been floating about in the air from all eternity, it might at last happen by chance that there would come a salad." "Yes," answered his wife, "but not so nice and well-dressed as mine." Atoms which have come together at random would not make such a beautiful universe.

The atom is mysterious. Life is mysterious. Scientists are far from having discovered their secrets. How much more then is God, the Creator of matter and life, mysterious. The Gospel according to John says, "No one has ever seen God" (John 1:18). When Moses once asked to see God's glory, he received the categorical answer: "You cannot see my face, for man shall not see me and live" (Exodus 33:20).

No philosopher can comprehend Him, but even the simplest man can apprehend Him, just as no scientist comprehends yet the secrets of the atom, but every man can handle matter constituted of atoms.

The New Testament tells us about this God, as does nature, too.

I once spoke with a prison officer, a member of the Communist party. He told me in a moment of confidence: "I looked one autumn day through the window at a bare tree. I knew that next spring it would again be full of leaves and buds, with birds chirping in its branches. And I adored the 'I do not know who' or 'I do not know what' which gives me trees and wheat and flowers. I throw black coals into the fire and the fire changes it into beautiful white flames. I adore the Power or the Person, I do not know who or what he is, which rewards our evil with good and sometimes changes ugly lives, lives of former bandits, into beautiful lives of martyrs of a holy cause. I have known such men among you Christians." This Communist officer did not comprehend God, but he apprehended Him.

It is easy for atheists to ridicule primitive conceptions of God —an old man with a white beard sitting on a throne, as He is depicted on icons.

When Christians are children, they are taught in a childlike way about God. Many of them, when they become older, fail to fulfill the biblical injunction to put away childish things. They remain with these childlike conceptions, which are easily mocked by the atheists. But God is other than some immature conception of Him.

These icon images are surely not more ridiculous than the image of the atom drawn by the great physicist Niels Bohr. The atom is otherwise than we can draw it, and God is otherwise than what we think of Him. But science could not do without its approximations. We Christians also use human words and human painting to express our feelings about God. But Thomas Aquinas, one of our great teachers, wrote, "God is not what you imagine or what you think you understand. If you understand, you have failed." Our mind is surely too small to encompass the Infinite Being, but —as I said—we can apprehend Him.

A Christian once asked an atheist, with whom he took a walk through the meadows, "Who made all these beautiful flowers?" "Forget it!" was the answer. "Do not come again with your stupid talk about God. The flowers exist by themselves." The Christian did not persist. After a few days, he was visited by this same atheist friend in his home. He had in his sitting room a beautiful picture representing flowers. The atheist asked him, "Who painted this?" The Christian said, "Do not begin with religious rubbish! Nobody painted these flowers. They came into the painting by themselves. Nature made the carved frame. Then by itself the picture jumped upon the wall, on to a nail which just happened to be there, driven by nobody. And that is all." The atheist took the joke badly. But then the Christian asked, "Is it logical to believe that these three flowers in the picture, which have no fragrance and no life, must have been created by somebody, while believing that the millions of living flowers with their heady perfume in the valleys and on the hills have no Creator?"

God is a mystery. Jesus teaches us to say: "Our Father in heaven" (Matthew 6:9), not "Our Father who walks on the streets and can be met by everybody on any corner." He is in the world incognito.

Pin a butterfly to a board and you have killed it. It is no more a butterfly, but its corpse. So we cannot pin down God in any definition. We use names for Him, knowing that they are inadequate. The utmost that we can say about Him is that He is the one beyond whom nothing greater can be conceived.

But God has revealed Himself in the person of Jesus Christ, the Son of God, who once came to this earth. About Him the New Testament speaks. Millions have had their lives changed by Him.

False is the assertion of *The Atheist's Handbook* that Christ's teachings destroy the joy of life. To renounce joy is un-Christian. Rejection of joy is a rejection of what we Christians consider the creation of God. Why should we refuse what a good Father has given us? The Old Testament provided that a man might vow to renounce for a short season all earthly pleasures. When this season was over, he had to bring a sacrifice to God as atonement for the sin of having disdained God's marvelous gift: pleasure. Christianity deprives nobody of joy. On the contrary, Christianity adds to pure earthly joys heavenly ones. What greater pleasure is there than to love?

Do not accept all these unproved falsehoods imputed to us, especially when Christian authors are not allowed to reply. The simple fact that atheists keep us gagged while they write shows that they are unfair and therefore not trustworthy.

Put your faith in God!

This God suffers with us. He shares all our sorrows. He sacrifices Himself for us. He desires us.

Marx and historical materialism have deprived reality of its very soul, God, and have thus devastated it.

The knowledge of God is the key for knowing the world profoundly. We do not have reality plus God, but reality clothed in the beauty of God. Similarly, in a painting we don't have scenery plus a sunset; rather, all the hills and valleys and trees are bathed in its colors.

In some caves of Thailand were discovered prehistoric drawings showing men and fish in what one might call "X-ray style." The artist of not less than 3,000 years ago shows the details which he could not see, but about the existence of which he knew. Drawing a man or an animal, he included the skeleton and such organs as the stomach, lungs, etc. Such drawings were found earlier among the aborigines of Australia.

We consider this type of art primitive. It might not be as beautiful as our art, but it is nearer to reality. In a gallery of portraits, what we see portrayed is not primarily the subjects themselves but rather the clothes made by their tailors. Of a subject we see only the face and hands. If nudes are exposed, we see the skin. We are content with very little. The primitive artist wished more of reality, because in a sense he was closer to reality than we sophisticated, modern men.

The New Testament speaks about the universe and history in the same "X-ray" manner. The materialists see only the outside of things. The believers see all the outside things, plus what animates the universe and history, the inside—God working in His creation and manifesting Himself as love in action.

God sent His own Son, Jesus Christ, on our behalf. As a baker takes upon himself your care for bread and the farmer your care for vegetables, as the shoemaker gives you his product, as a professor takes away your ignorance and gives you knowledge accumulated over the centuries, so Jesus, the Son of God, the only one who never committed any sin, has taken it upon Himself to care for you. He gives you His righteousness. You become like a newborn babe, like a man who has never sinned. Life begins anew in fellowship with God. As for your sinfulness, He has taken it upon Himself.

You feel, somehow, that your sins have been very grave. They have produced suffering in others. Perhaps tears and blood have been shed, and you are guilty. Well, Jesus bore not only your sins, but also the punishment for your sins. He bore it, dying on the cross on a mount called Golgotha near Jerusalem. Through His wounds we are healed.

The New Testament says, "God so loved the world, that he gave his only Son, that whoever believes in him should not perish but have eternal life" (John 3:16). Note the word "whoever," even atheists; anyone—even men who have committed the worst of crimes.

The New Testament teaches us that Jesus is standing at the door of our heart and constantly knocking. If anyone hears Him and opens the door, He comes in and talks with Him heart to heart.

Life does not consist only in working for the state or in eating, drinking, and enjoying sex. Christ is a spiritual being. He desires to enable you to overcome sin and death and hell and only waits for your decision. And He promises not only a future heaven, but a heavenly life right now in your soul.

The New Testament tells us that Christ, the Son of God, loved men so much that He prayed for His murderers even while enduring the pains of the cross. You may have been a thief. Christ died among thieves and, while hanging on the cross, saved one of them, who repented, for Paradise. He did not shun scoundrels or harlots. It was His greatest joy to forgive great crimes.

The New Testament is deprecated by atheists, because it proclaims love as the guiding principle of life and makes one's heart a corner of heaven. The mind begins to think truthfully, because errors in life are often nothing less than a lack of love. After you have looked earnestly into the mirror of truth, which is Christ, great compassion toward all mankind will fill your soul and you will be wonderfully free.

The Soviet population was not permitted to know the message of the New Testament, because it would reconcile them to God. Therefore, the fierce but unfounded attacks upon it. But it is easy for us Christians, who have this deep insight into the great realities of sin and atonement, to understand why our atheist friends shudder before the cross and even write a book 700 pages long against it. With unwelcome intuition the atheists feel that the Bible contains the final truth.

Stalin is dead, but never will any Communist sing, "Stalin, lover of my soul"; nor is he apt to sing, "Khrushchev, my most beloved"; nor will his descendants a century from now sing to Brezhnev, "I need thee every hour."

Yet these are sung about Jesus all over the world almost two thousand years after His crucifixion.

The Communists were never able to silence these songs in holy Mother Russia!

About them no songs will be sung.

Already, jokes told about them today show what fame they will have in the future.

There is much sadness in the world. It needs laughter. I like it so much when people are joyful that I don't mind if they laugh at my expense. I hope that my opponents have the same feelings and that they will not take it amiss if I tell them two jokes which circulated in Russia.

The first: A high school pupil was asked in history class, "Who was Stalin?" He answered, "A man who, loving the cult of his own personality, became a murderer. He killed even his nearest comrades. This is the teaching about him of the Twentieth Congress of our Party."

"Bravo," says the professor. "Now, answer, please, who was Khrushchev?"

Promptly, the boy replied, "Khrushchev was an idiot, righteously removed from leadership by the vote of the Central Committee."

"Also very well. Now for the last question: Who is Brezhnev?"

"He is another idiot," came the answer.

The professor stopped him: "This will probably be true in a year or two, when a corresponding resolution is taken. For the time being, he is a genial leader, and I have to give you a bad mark."

And a second joke: In a school a teacher told the children, "The Party is our father, and the Red Army is our mother." Then he asked one of the children, "What would you like to become?" The child answered, "An orphan."

Men have loved Jesus. Others have hated Him. Most have been indifferent to His message. But nobody has ever dared to make malicious jokes about Him.

14

IRREVERENT ATTACKS AGAINST THE BIBLE

From criticism of the New Testament, *The Atheist's Handbook* passes to criticism of the whole Bible.

We are sorry that here also the attacks are vulgar and shallow. We could have expected otherwise. There is such a thing as an elegant, generous form of disbelief.

Such, for example, is the atheism of Ludwig Feuerbach. He did not believe in God but wanted to keep religion, which makes man noble, loving, and righteous. In *The Essence of Christianity*, Feuerbach called religion "holy" because it is "the tradition of the first consciousness," which to him meant childhood. Is it not beautiful to keep the memories of the childish period of mankind, he asks?

Jesus would not have objected to calling religion childish. He taught us to become like little children. We all value the remembrances of childhood. Why throw them out as many atheists do? Is it because they are reminded of a time when their souls were more beautiful than they are now?

We would recommend that our opponents read *The Atheist's Mass* by Honore de Balzac. The chief character is an atheistic surgeon, Desplein. When he was a very poor and hungry student, a water-carrier named Bourgeat, animated by Christian love, had helped him, through hard work and personal sacrifice, to finish his studies, after which the latter became a renowned doctor.

Now Desplein was an infidel. But when Bourgeat, from his deathbed, requested him to say mass for the repose of his soul, the atheist professor, impelled by gratitude, agreed to comply. Thereafter, he regularly said the required prayers for the deceased Catholic who had done him good.

We have attempted to show understanding for atheists, but we feel we have a right to expect cultured atheists to recognize the extent to which their culture depends on the Bible and to be at least decent in their attacks.

Friedrich Nietzsche was the first to declare that "God is dead." He was Hitler's favorite philosopher. Hitler drew the right conclusions. If God were dead, Hitler need have no scruples about killing millions of innocent men and even children. But Nietzsche was far removed from his future disciple. Nietzsche spoke about the death of God with holy awe. His madman, after proclaiming the death of God, goes to different churches and sings a *Requiem aeternam Deo*, a hymn of mourning for the dead God. To Nietzsche, God was dead. For him, this conclusion was a source of high drama. But one can sense that he was genuinely sorry that his god was no longer alive.

Many atheists, on the contrary, revel in the death of God. Now they no longer have to worry about conscience, truthfulness, and love. They can do what they like.

This atheism is indecent.

R. Garaudy, one-time member of the Central Committee of the Communist Party of France, wrote, "We cannot disregard the essential contribution of Christianity without getting poorer" (*Anathema to Dialogue*).

Lunacharsky, once a minister of education in the Soviet government, wrote, "The notion of God always contains something eternally beautiful... Sorrow always dwells in men. He who does not know how to conceive the world religiously is condemned to pessimism..."

Some atheists begin the history of right thought with themselves, with catastrophic results. They end up ignoring or seeking to obliterate truth acquired by mankind during millenniums of development.

Consequently, they make a caricature of religion. We regret this. Caricatures are always dangerous for those who draw them.

A young woman once had a discussion with the great satirist Hogarth while he was at the drawing board. She expressed a wish to learn to draw caricatures, to which Hogarth replied, "Alas, young lady, it is not a faculty to be envied. Take my advice and never draw caricatures. By the long practice of it, I have lost the enjoyment of beauty. I never see a face but what it is distorted. I never have the satisfaction of beholding the human face divine."

Those who caricature true religion are in the same situation. In the distorting mirror of their warped minds, even angels seem to have the devil's features.

They do not realize that if the Bible were set aside as a valueless book, all the famous literature of the world would perish with it. What would remain of Dostoevsky, Tolstoy, Milton, John Bunyan, Walter Scott, and Anatole France? Tennyson said that the Book of Job was the finest poem he had ever read. There are three hundred quotations from the Bible in his works. Shakespeare used over five hundred ideas and phrases taken from it. Byron's poem "Darkness" was inspired by the Book of Jeremiah.

Even *Das Kapital* by Marx would have to be changed, along with his other writings and those of Engels, because they are saturated with references to the Bible.

If the Bible were taken away, the works of Michelangelo, Leonardo da Vinci, Raphael, Rembrandt, and many other great painters of the world would be unintelligible to us, as would many of the great pieces of music of Bach, Beethoven, Mozart, Haydn, Brahms, and others.

Listen to the testimony of renowned men.

William Gladstone, four-time premier of Great Britain, said, "If asked what is the remedy for the deeper sorrows of the human heart, what a man should chiefly look to in his progress as the power that is to sustain him under trials and enable him to confront his inevitable afflictions, I must point him to something which in a well-known hymn is called 'The Old, Old Story' told in an old book, which is the greatest and best gift ever given to mankind." He referred to the Bible.

Jean Jacques Rousseau writes, "How mean, how contemptible are the words of our philosophers with all their contradictions, compared with the Scriptures. Is it possible that a book at once so simple and so sublime should be merely the words of man?"

Goethe writes, "The Bible becomes ever more beautiful, the more it is understood."

Heinrich Heine, who was very far from being a religious enthusiast, writes, "The depth of creation written into the blue mysteries of heaven; sunrise and sunset; promise and fulfillment; birth and death; the whole human drama—everything is in this book. It is a book of books, the Bible."

The English and German languages in a particular way would not be what they are if they had not been transformed by the Bible. It is the one book which has provided the impetus for giving hundreds of peoples and tribes their first alphabet. Through the labors of dedicated men and women, it is the first book they learn to read.

Garibaldi, the Italian patriot who politically liberated and unified his fatherland (finishing this work in 1870), said of the Bible: "This is the cannon that will make Italy free."

Below is the testimony of some of America's most renowned presidents:

Washington: "Above all, the pure and unbending light of Revelation has had illuminating influence on mankind and increased the blessings of society."

Lincoln: "I have always taken counsel of God and referred to Him my plans and have never adopted a course of proceeding without being assured as far as I could be of His approval. I should be the most presumptuous blockhead upon this footstone, if I for one day thought that I could discharge the duties which have come upon me since I came into this place, without the aid and enlightenment of One who is wiser and stronger than others."

Grant: "Hold fast to the Bible as the sheet anchor of your liberties; write its precepts in your hearts, and practice them in your lives. To the influence of this Book are we indebted for all the progress made in true civilization, and to this we must look as our guide in the future."

Garfield: "Choose the undying Jesus as your everlasting friend and helper. Follow him, not simply as a Nazarene, the man of Galilee, but as an ever-living spiritual person, full of love and com-passion, who will stand by you in life and death and eternity. The hopes of the world are false, but as the vine lives in the branches, so Christ lives in the Christian, and he shall never die."

McKinley: "We must be doers, not hearers only. To be doers of the word it is necessary that we must first be hearers of the word; yet attendance at church is not enough. We must study the Bible, but let it not rest there. We must apply it in active life."

Wilson: "If every man in the United States would read a chap-ter of the Bible every day, most of our national problems would disappear."

Franklin D. Roosevelt: "I reiterate the statement which I have made times before—that a revival of religion is what this country most needs; that in such a revival we would find a solution of all our problems, whether political, economic, or social."

Even the atheist Marx wrote: "Luther, by giving the Bible to the people in the vernacular language, put into their hands a pow-erful weapon against the nobility, the landlords, and the clergy."

Stalin and Mikoyan were both seminarians. The latter even has a degree in theology. It was the Bible which formed the beginning of their culture. Khrushchev confessed publicly that he learned to read from the Bible.

The essential idea of every socialist constitution—"If anyone is not willing to work, let him not eat"—is copied textually from the Bible (2 Thessalonians 3:10).

The idea of communism was taken from the Bible, in which we are told:

> Now the full number of those who believed [in Jesus] were of one heart and soul, and no one said that any of the things that belonged to him was his own, but they had everything in common... There was not a needy person among them, for as many as were owners of lands or houses sold them and brought the proceeds of what was sold and laid it at the apostles' feet, and it was distributed to each as any had need. (Acts 4:32–35)

The first disciples of Jesus lived under communism, but a communism based on love and free will. Nobody was pressured, nor was anything expropriated. Love prompted everyone to share with his brother. In spite of dissimilarities, today's communism was also of biblical origin.

I can accept the fact that a person might not believe in the Bible, but that should not prevent him from respecting his heritage. Does it count for nothing that the Bible was the first book printed in Europe? Does it count for nothing that Christian missionaries taught the natives of Africa to give up cannibalism, to read, to behave as civilized men?

A former cannibal once said to an atheist, "What? This book is not true? I take it in my house and sit down and read it, and it makes my heart burst with joy. How can this be a lie? I was an eater of men, a drunkard, thief, and liar, and the book spoke to me and made of me a new man. No, this book is not a lie."

The educated atheists would have been eaten by the natives in many parts of the world if the missionaries had not taught them first the Christian religion. While spreading atheism, these propagandists should be thankful to Christianity for creating civilization and providing the freedom for them to operate.

An honorable atheist is one who bows before the church in gratitude for what mankind owes to Christianity. But to spit in the well from which you and the whole civilized world have drunk is terribly wrong.

In the seventeenth century, when atheism was rare among Jews, a Jew told a rabbi, "I don't believe in God." The rabbi embraced the man and said, "How I envy you, brother. You are in a much better spiritual state than I. When I see a man suffering, I say to myself, 'God will help him,' and don't give him assistance. You don't believe in the existence of God, so you have to help him. You have to do the deeds which God would do if he were to exist. Just go on like this: feed the hungry, comfort the distressed, give truth and joy to those in need, embrace everybody in love, and in general behave as God would behave if he existed. And then come back in a year and tell me if there is a God or not."

The rabbi could afford to take an elegant attitude toward the atheist, in order to encourage him to squeeze the best out of his atheism. Some atheists do not behave like this toward a believer.

They live on a lower level and their whole stand is untenable.

They appeal to our reason, trying with arguments to prove their point. Now, if the atheists admit that we can reason, why was it impossible to find a Bible in any bookshop in the Soviet Union? The population should have been able to read it for themselves, compare it with what its opponents have to say, and then draw their own conclusions. Why was the Bible banned? Did they not believe in man's power to reason "rightly"? Then why go to the trouble to adduce arguments? Just give the order "Disbelieve!" and be done with it.

15

DID THE CHARACTERS IN THE BIBLE REALLY EXIST?

Criticism of the Bible text is a legitimate concern of the human mind. Christian theologians did not need to wait for the advice of atheists to verify biblical history, reconciling biblical and secular chronologies and investigating archaeological data. The fact that we believe in the divine inspiration and the infallibility of Scriptures has never prevented us from examining minutely its text and its content, to be very sure we have the words as God inspired them, unmarred by later copyists or translators.

The Bible criticism as practiced by our atheist opponents is of an entirely different type. They deny the most important events of Bible narrative and relegate the principal biblical personalities to the realm of myth.

But the facts of the Bible remain, and science cannot confute them. It is a fact that the archaeologist's shovel always substantiates, never disproves, the biblical narrative.

For the atheists and liberal theologians, Adam and Eve are personalities of a myth.

There is no valid reason to deny the biblical record that Adam and Eve really lived on earth in the garden of Eden and were expelled from it, just as we do not uncritically discard other historical records kept by mankind.

But our opponents render us a service by calling the story a myth. A myth is not necessarily something unreal, but is, rather, highest reality expressed in images and symbols arising from, and appealing to, the depths of the human soul.

The story of Adam and Eve is more than history. It is history and myth at the same time.

Your own lives, my dear opponents, are a reproduction of what happened to Adam and Eve. There has been the innocence of childhood in a world untrammeled with worries and fretting about big problems. Perhaps you remember when intentional sin, trespassing against the moral law you lived by, first invaded your life and made you hide from God. Later it may have taken the form of hiding some of your autobiography from the public. We should not reproach our first forefathers. If Adam and Eve had not sinned, *we* would have eaten the forbidden fruit.

Adam and Eve are archetypes of general human experience, of what happens with every soul. Myths cannot be opposed to reality. They are very often a deepening of the sense of some isolated fact, showing it to be typical for the whole of mankind. You cannot disregard the value of the *Mona Lisa* by saying that it is only a portrait. It is the portrait of a living being. A portrait is as much a reality as the human being it shows. The *Mona Lisa* is, in a certain sense, even more real than the person it portrays. It is more beautiful, more permanent; it sums up her best features. It corrects nature. The portrait does not contradict the person. The spiritual sense of Adam and Eve's story does not contradict their being historical beings.

What I said about Adam and Eve applies also to the remedy for sin, to the sacrifice of Christ. Every man who has done something wrong seeks a scapegoat, someone he can charge with his own offense. Knowing this psychological law embedded in the sinner, Christ offered Himself as the scapegoat. He, being the Son of God, takes the whole responsibility for our entire life, good and evil. He has identified Himself with us out of love and has borne our punishment. What He endured in the crucifixion on Golgotha avails us as if we ourselves had passed through all His torments. We are free from our sins and guilt because Christ shed His blood for us. Then He rose from the dead, showing us that we who believe in Him will also be resurrected to be with Him in Paradise.

His death and resurrection are historic reality. But the myth about a god who dies as a sacrifice for sin and rises again goes back before Christ. Atheists are correct in reminding us that approximately the same things were believed about the god Horus of the Egyptians, of the god Mithra, and others. Unlike Christ, these gods were not historic, but archetypal realities. All these "gods" were counterfeits of the genuine Redeemer who had been promised to mankind, and in that sense foreshadowed the coming of Christ. Horus and Mithra and Dionysus were names given to the Savior after whom mankind longed.

We will not worry, then, if our opponents call Adam and Eve and the Redeemer promised to them after the fall in Paradise myths.

A flood in Noah's time which destroyed the whole earth? Another legend, atheists say.

But the biblical narrative is corroborated by the Chinese, Greek, British, and Mexican stories of a deluge. Cuneiform tablets unearthed in Babylonia in 1870 also bore an account of the flood, striking because of its resemblance to the Bible record. Believed to date from 3000 BC, these tablets must have been written when people vividly recalled the deluge.

Called the Gilgamesh epic, this narrative tells how the hero of the flood, Utnapishtim, escaped the general destruction of mankind. The great gods of the ancient city of Shuruppak (modern Fara) resolved to destroy the race by a flood. The god Ea disclosed the divine decree to Utnapishtim and saved him and his family.

Another story of the flood has been found written in Sumerian, a language which precedes both Assyrian and Babylonian.

The renowned anthropologist Sir James Frazer collected traditions about the flood from the most varied and remote places, such as the Leeward Islands, Bengal, China, and Malaysia. Everywhere peoples and backward tribes keep the memory of this tremendous event. They agree that the flood was a punishment for grave sins and that only a few righteous people were saved.

Josephus Flavius is generally considered one of the most reliable historians of antiquity. He writes in *Antiquities of the Jews*, "The Armenians call this place (where Noah and his family came out of the ark) *Apobaterion*, the place of descent."

In the story of the flood, facts and myth merge again. Engraved in the deepest reaches of our mind is the truth that generalized grave sin will result in catastrophe. We know also that there have been many cases when the righteousness of a few has miraculously saved them from general destruction. The historical account of the flood was overlaid in the memories of many peoples with legends which express this truth. These legends are as real as the flood itself.

The flood in Noah's time was not a unique event. Jesus says, "For as were the days of Noah, so will be the coming of the Son of Man. For as in those days before the flood they were eating and drinking, marrying and giving in marriage, until the day when Noah entered the ark, and they were unaware until the flood came and swept them all away, so will be the coming of the Son of Man" (Matthew 24:37–39).

The world is now on the brink of a new catastrophe for sinners. In 2 Peter 3:10, the Bible says that this time it will be destroyed by fire. ("The elements will melt with fervent heat," NKJV. These words were written two thousand years ago by Peter the fisherman long before anyone knew about chemical elements, or the destructive power and annihilating capacity of atomic fission and its fervent heat.) As Noah had a warning from God, so the church has a warning today. The world in Noah's time was destroyed, although its wickedness was not sufficient to forbid Noah's preaching. What judgment can today's world expect when, in some parts of the world, it puts a prohibition upon the warnings! Mankind should not be aware of the dangers facing the world of today;

therefore they deny the flood of old—even at the price of denying historical evidence.

There is no proof for the existence of Abraham and his descendants, say our opponents further.

Has any historical excavation proved the existence of Spartacus, the leader of a revolt of slaves, a man who figures in all histories of socialism? Surely not. It is taken for granted that Spartacus really existed because a Roman historian wrote about him. Then why do the historians of socialism not apply the same yardstick to biblical personalities, even if historical excavations should not prove anything about their existence? Why should they have spoken about Abraham who lived most of his life as a nomad? We believe in his historical existence, as we believe in the historical reality of Spartacus, because historians, the writers of the Bible, speak about his life and the lives of the other personalities of the Old Testament.

Further, all the Jews of all times have known themselves to be the descendants of Abraham, Isaac, and Jacob. All the Arabs from time immemorial have known that Abraham was their father. All the Christians and all the Muslims of the world have always venerated Abraham as the ancestor of their faith in one single God.

Should all this count for nothing?

Abraham bought the cave of Machpelah for the burial of Sarah. Afterward, this cave became a family tomb. There were buried Isaac, Rebekah, Leah, and Jacob. A mosque and a synagogue now stand above this cave, and it is one of the holiest places of pilgrimage for the Muslims.

Imagine that after a few hundred or thousand years someone seeing the mausoleum of Lenin should say that Lenin was not a historical personality but a myth. The corpse of Lenin, it would be said, is only a wax figure. Suppose that after two thousand years archaeologists who had heard about Stalin should find nothing relating to him, not a corpse nor even so much as a wax figure. Surely they would deny his existence.

"How foolish," you say. But then the denial of Abraham's existence is also foolish.

A site in Israel indicates the historicity of Abraham's grandson. The well of Jacob, where Jesus spoke with the Samaritan woman, still exists in Palestine and is covered by a little Greek church. The well itself is immediately below the high altar.

But Jacob and his descendants are also not historical personages, we are told by skeptics. Either they are ignorant, or else they are deliberately hiding the truth.

In Tell Hariri in 1933 excavations were made by the well-known archaeologist, Professor Parrot. Tell Hariri is between Damascus and Mosul in the very place from which the family of Abraham is reported to have come to Canaan. Now the Mari civilization had been discovered there, and the Assyriologists were able to decipher a clay tablet. It was a report of Bannum, an officer of the desert police, which is dated around the seventeenth century BC. The report has the following wording: "Say to my Lord this from Bannum, thy servant: Yesterday I left Mari and spent the night at Zuruban. All the Benjamites were sending fire signals. From Samanum to Ilum-Muluk, from Ilum-Muluk to Mishlam all the

Benjamite villages in the Terqua district replied with fire signals; I am not yet certain what these signals meant."

In addition, the chronological tables discovered in that place mention the Benjamites three times. "The year in which Iahdulim went to Hen and laid hands upon the territory of the Benjamites" is an inscription from the reign of King Iahdulim. From the reign of the last monarch of Mari, we have two inscriptions: "The year that Zimri-lim killed the Dawidum of the Benjamites," and "The year after Zimri-lim killed the Dawidum of the Benjamites."

Benjamin is, according to the Bible, Jacob's youngest son. How then can skeptics say that the sons of Jacob are not historical persons?

The first time that the name Israel occurs in non-biblical documents is on an inscription, now in the Cairo museum, from a mortuary temple near Thebes, on which the victory of Pharaoh Mezemptah over the Libyans is commemorated. In order to augment his triumph, other notable victories which this ruler is said to have achieved are also mentioned. The end of the hymn of praise is as follows: "Canaan is despoiled and all its evil with it. Askelon is taken captive. Gezer is conquered. Yanoam is blotted out. The people of Israel are desolate; Israel has no offspring. Palestine has become a widow for Egypt."

So the name of Israel is already historical by the year 1229 BC.

The ruler of that time boasted of destroying the Jews, just as his follower Nasser boasted, before he was defeated by Israel, which will never be utterly destroyed.

It surely seems to be a very ridiculous thing to write a book of 700 pages to prove that over 4,000 years ago a man with the name of Abraham did not exist, that he had no descendants with the names of Isaac, Jacob, and Benjamin, and that the whole biblical story about the people of Israel is untrue. Many atheists are not interested in their own ancestors of 4,500 years ago. Why should they be interested in denying specifically that the Jews have a history dating from a man named Abraham?

The denial has a deep sense. It will best be explained by a joke, which must be Jewish, since we are discussing the Jews.

Goldstein was riding in a train. Opposite him was another Jew, Hershcovici. They did not know each other. Goldstein wanted to enter into a conversation, so he asked Hershcovici, "Comrade, tell me, please, what time it is." Hershcovici did not answer. The question was repeated several times, every time in a louder voice. It did not help. In the end, Goldstein said, "But, comrade, I see that you have a watch on your wrist. Why don't you tell me the time?"

Hershcovici replied: "Comrade, you are not interested in this. I surmise that you would like to chat a little bit. If I had told you that it was 9 o'clock, you would have asked, 'What brand of watch do you have?' I would have replied, 'It is a Swiss gold watch.' You would have answered, 'Then you must have a high position. You could not afford such a watch otherwise.' I would have replied, 'Yes, I am a director in the Ministry of External Commerce.' Then you would have asked me where I stay in Moscow. I would answer, 'On Street Artileriinaia.' You would have asked if I have a family. I would have told you that I have a wife and three daughters.

You would have asked if by chance I had their picture with me. I would have said yes and would have shown you the picture. You would have liked my beautiful elder daughter Esther and would have asked me if I would allow you to visit me once. Politeness would have obliged me to answer yes. You would have fallen in love with Esther and would have asked her hand in marriage. And why should I give my daughter in marriage to a man who does not even possess a watch?"

The existence of Abraham and his descendants must be denied, because if atheists were to admit that Abraham existed, according to the biblical record and all the traditions of hundreds of millions of Jews, Christians, and Muslims, we would have asked why Abraham was so conspicuous that his name should remain alive in history after four millennia. The only reply could be that he is famous because he believed God, followed His commands, and was ready to sacrifice even his dearest son for Him. To which we would have asked whether Abraham ever met God. The answer is that he often heard the voice of God speaking to him clearly. We would be interested to know what God told him. The answer would be that, among other things, God told him that He wanted to make a covenant with him. In his seed, that is, through one of his offspring, all nations would be blessed. Now, since everyone wishes to have a blessed life, we would have asked the name of this descendant of Abraham who was to impart happiness. The reply is simple: The New Testament begins by telling us that Jesus is this descendant of Abraham. We would have asked how anybody can receive blessings from Him. And we would hear the message of the gospel: Jesus died on the cross for us sinners. He bore the punishment for our offenses. Whoever believes in Him is cleansed from all his sins and has eternal life now and in Paradise.

The authors of *The Atheist's Handbook* therefore proceed carefully, as did comrade Hershcovici in the joke. They cut the discussion short. The biblical personalities never existed. They have the watch on the wrist but will not say what time it is.

This is their purpose also in other denials of biblical truth. This is their purpose in finding fault with the Bible and seeking contradictions in it.

16

DELIVERY OF THE JEWS FROM EGYPTIAN SLAVERY

The Bible says that the Jews were slaves in Egypt, but that God delivered them from bondage with a mighty hand, doing miracles for them. The Egyptians who pursued them were drowned in the Red Sea. This biblical story is surely dangerous for slaveholders. It might suggest to slaves, to men who live under a dictatorship, that God is in favor of the emancipation of slaves.

Therefore, this page of history has to be wiped out, too. The authors of *The Atheist's Handbook* graciously assure us that all this is sheer fiction. They write:

> For a century and a half, there have been archaeological excavations in Egypt which were made with great thoroughness, but in a good number of monuments which were discovered, in the multitude of inscriptions which have been

deciphered, in pictorial images and those of other
nature, there is nothing found to confirm the
Biblical legend about the Egyptian slavery.

Is it right for them to make such a criticism of the Bible?

My honorable opponents again show a lack of archaeological
knowledge.

They do not know about the inscribed stone of the time of
Ramses II, found at Beisan in 1923, stating that he employed
captive Semites (in the Tell-el-Amarna tablets the Hebrews appear
under the name "Khabiri") to build a city named after him.

The sun-dried bricks of the store cities, which can be seen in
the Cairo museum, are stamped with the words "Ramses." You can
see that some of them are bound with straw, others only with stub-
ble, and finally, some of them are made without any straw or other
binding substance. All this corroborates the decree of Pharaoh as
recorded in the biblical Book of Exodus, giving the command that
the Israelites should no longer be supplied with straw.

The Bible says that ten plagues were sent by God upon the
Egyptians to induce them to let the Jewish slaves go. The last
plague was the death of all first-born, beginning with the first-born
of Pharaoh, who sat on his throne.

If the assertion of the Bible is correct, the son of Amenhotep
the Second, the Pharaoh during the Exodus, must have died in
that judgment. Amenhotep the Second himself died in 1423 BC,
and he was followed by Thotmes the Fourth. On a large red granite
block which is placed between the feet of the sphinx of Ghizeh is

carved what is called the dream inscription of Thotmes the Fourth. In this, we are told that this future Pharaoh when young fell asleep and dreamed that a sphinx came to him and startled him with the prophecy that he would one day become King of Egypt.

Since the law of primogeniture held good in Egypt, he could not have been Amenhotep's eldest son, or the hopes of his accession would not have been so remote that he would be amazed by the promise of the sphinx. So the first-born of Pharaoh must have died in the tenth plague.

Is this not a strange confirmation of the biblical account?

Ancient Egyptian history is quite well-known. There are many records. But not a one speaks about the disappearance of the Egyptian army and its king in the sea, skeptics point out.

I would like to know which nation has ever been keen about registering its defeats. When the Soviet army retreated from the borders to Stalingrad, Stalin did not publicize the defeats. Neither did the Germans publicize theirs when the tide turned. The Egyptian historians cared as little about objective truth as their modern counterparts.

In this matter we do not have the Egyptian side of the story. That is all. But we have the Bible, which tells not only the Jewish side, but God's words and God's wonders. There is no reason to disbelieve the wonderful deliverance of the slaves, though it may be unpleasant for slaveholders and their flatterers.

In the imperial palace in Tokyo are kept three signs of the Japanese empire—a very old sword, a diamond, and a mirror of the great king. On the back of this mirror are inscribed some letters which have only recently been deciphered in Japan. After the Second World War, a brother of the emperor, the Prince Takahito Mikasa, began to inquire into Judaism. When the emperor was visited by Rabbi Goldmann of the Beth-Israel temple in Hertford, who was the executive chairman of the National Jewish Welfare Commission, the prince took care that the Rabbi should see this mirror of the great emperor. Without any difficulty the Rabbi was able to identify the letters as the Hebrew words Ehjeh Asher Ehjeh—I AM WHO I AM. The very words of the Bible, as found in Exodus 3:14!

Immediately the prince and the rabbi began to speculate about how these Jewish words recorded by Moses in the Bible came to be found on an ancient sacred object of the Japanese. They supposed that in times of old, during the Babylonian captivity of the Jews, members of the ten tribes of Israel had brought this mirror as a present to the ruling emperor.

In 1941, the Japanese bishop Jujai Nakada published a book called Japan in the Bible. Relying on documents of ancient times, he says that in the year AD 216, one hundred thousand men came from the Middle East to Japan. They are called in Japanese history the Hata tribe, and they won a very great influence over the economy and culture of Japan. The Hata called themselves Israj, which is much akin to Israel. They spoke about a great leader, whom they called prince Hata Kawa Katsu, who as a babe was rescued from the water, was then brought up in the palace of the king, and eventually freed from the bondage of slavery. In this form the biblical story of Moses came to Japan.

The extra-biblical proofs of history as recorded by the Holy Scriptures are too numerous to be mentioned. They certainly cannot be discarded.

17

CONTRADICTIONS IN THE BIBLE

Atheists mention contradictions in the Bible.

In 2 Samuel 8:4 it is written that David, in a fight with Hadadezer, took from him seven hundred horsemen, whereas in 1 Chronicles 18:4 it says that David took captive seven thousand horsemen. Our honored adversaries cannot reconcile these two different statements.

What would they say if they found a history of the Second World War in which it was claimed that in the battle for Kiev a hundred thousand Russian prisoners were taken, whereas fifty pages later it was asserted that in the battle at Kiev only ten thousand Russians fell prisoner?

The explanation is simple. During the last great war there were three battles for Kiev. The number of prisoners differed in these battles. Why must we presume, then, that in these two different books of the Bible the same battle against Hadadezer is described?

Another criticism of the Bible: It declares that King David "did what was right in the eyes of the LORD and did not turn aside from anything that he commanded him all the days of his life" (1 Kings 15:5). But did he not sin? The Bible itself records elsewhere what grave crimes he committed.

He surely did sin, but these sins were forgiven and atoned for, and therefore they did not count any longer before God. They were forgotten. The marvel is that a sinner who has repented is righteous before God, and therefore it is within the context of God's lovingkindness that the Scriptures record such beautiful words about David. The forgiven sinner is, in the sight of God, whiter than snow.

Let our atheist friends repent, and they too will be forgiven!

The authors of *The Atheist's Handbook* are very happy at having made the discovery that the apostle called Thaddeus in Matthew's Gospel is called Judas the son of James in the Book of Luke. What a grave error! But let us turn the tables on them. How do they reconcile the fact that a certain Ulianov is generally referred to as Lenin, and that the Djugashvili of one biographer is the Stalin of another?

Our opponents discover in the Bible a multitude of such "contradictions." They are not worth being considered.

Thus, for example, they point out that Jesus once told His disciples to sell even their clothes in order to buy themselves swords. On the other hand, when Peter tried to defend Jesus with his sword, He said to him, "Put your sword back into its place" (Matthew 26:52). Jesus did not wish to be defended. His desire was to die for the sins of the world.

Now Jesus' instruction to sell their garments and buy swords was given after the last supper when He was on His way to

Gethsemane, knowing He would be arrested. Since it was late in the evening and the disciples had no opportunity to buy anything, He obviously was not telling them to purchase swords for immediate use. Instead, He is warning His disciples that for many centuries they will have great dangers to face and that they should be prepared to defend themselves and the cause of righteousness. The sword He is referring to here is the "sword of the Spirit, which is the word of God" (Ephesians 6:17). This is the sword Christians are to use to pierce men's hearts.

He who is not prepared to defend a righteous cause does not love it. Every mother who loves her child will fight tooth and nail to protect him against an intruder who plans to kidnap or kill him.

When one of the disciples seeks to reassure Jesus with the words, "Here are two swords," Jesus replies with a touch of irony, "It is enough" (Luke 22:38). The time will come for His disciples to understand Him better.

Skeptical critics have found another contradiction in Luke's Gospel: They note that since the people were on the side of Jesus, the chief priests had to think of ways to kill Him secretly so that His sympathizers could not rally to His defense, whereas a few days later, the mob cries, "Crucify him, crucify him!" (John 19:6). Our opponents say that such a radical change in the temper of the local populace virtually overnight was not possible; therefore, the story told by the evangelist Luke cannot be true.

What a pity that they are not good students of history.

There was a morning in Moscow when all the radio stations began their programs with the singing of hymns of praise to Stalin, just as they had done for twenty years. The newspapers on that morning were also full of the same praises. It was the day when the twentieth congress of the Communist Party of the Soviet Union began. During that day, Khrushchev delivered a speech saying that Stalin, whom the whole nation and he himself had flattered for decades as the greatest genius, was in reality a mass murderer and torturer, not only of his adversaries, but even of his own comrades. In no time, the whole Russian people turned against the erstwhile providential leader and, instead of singing his praises, found ways to ridicule him. Soon even his corpse was removed from the tomb.

The state of mind of the populace changes very quickly. So it was in the case of one of mankind's most degraded leaders, Joseph Stalin, and so it was in the case of the most beautiful exemplar of mankind, Jesus of Nazareth.

Human nature is the same in all ages; the alleged contradictions exist not in the Gospels but in the minds and hearts of man.

The contention that Judas did not need to give the soldiers who had come to arrest Jesus a sign of recognition is ridiculous, even childish. Because Palestine is a very small country and Jesus had traveled widely throughout Galilee and Judea, that is no reason to believe that His face was widely recognized. Today's major personalities are known because their pictures are published in newspapers and they appear on television, but in those days no such mass media existed. So there must have been thousands of men who, while they had heard of Jesus, had never seen Him face to face. The Roman soldiers and the servants of Caiaphas the high priest had probably never been very keen to listen to Jesus' sermons, any more than the officers of the Communist secret police would be anxious to hear today's preachers in Communist countries, except for sinister purposes. So it was natural that someone should provide a sure sign of recognition of the person to be arrested. Furthermore, the encounter was in the dark of night, with only flickering torches to light the faces of a dozen weary, undistinguished men, and positive identification was required.

The authors of *The Atheist's Handbook* despise Jesus for exhibiting fear in the Garden of Gethsemane, where He was arrested, and despairing on the cross.

To possess great virtues is surely very beautiful. To hide these virtues as trees hide their fruit beneath the leaves is much more commendable. The aim of Christ was to open a way toward heaven for the weakest ones, to show that even they are acceptable to God. In order to build such a bridge, He must not play the hero. If His actions had appeared heroic and unattainable in all circumstances, we average and below-average men could never have taken Him as a pattern of life. Therefore, He descended to the level of our human weakness, praying in Gethsemane, "Father,... remove this cup from me" (Luke 22:42), and crying on the cross, "My God, my God, why have you forsaken me?" (Matthew 27:46). He did this so that we, who often sink in despair and wish that the cup of bitter fate would be taken away from us, should find in Him a trustworthy friend. That was the aim of Christ's behavior. To call it cowardice is not right.

Atheists speak about some contradictions between the Old and the New Testaments.

They point out that in the Gospel according to John, it is written that nobody has ever seen God, whereas in the Old Testament the patriarch Jacob says, "I have seen God face to face" (Genesis 32:30).

The explanation is very simple.

The Hebrew language in biblical times was very poor and therefore contained many homonyms. The same word had many senses. The word "God" in that time meant first of all the Creator of heaven and earth. The word was used also for Christ. Angelic beings are several times called gods in the Old Testament, as are even men. The Creator says to Moses, "I have made you like God to Pharaoh" (Exodus 7:1), and in one of the psalms, the Jews, as members of a chosen people, are told, "You are gods" (Psalm 82:6). So when Jacob said, "I have seen God face to face," he meant an angelic being, whereas John speaks about God in the highest sense of the word—the last reality, the Creator of heaven and earth.

But enough!

Atheists look at the Bible from below, from a human standpoint. From this angle, it is really a puzzle. Take some beautiful embroidery, look at it on the wrong side, and it is a senseless zigzag of threads. You must look on the other side to find its beauty. So the Scriptures are not to be looked at from below, from the standpoint of man, who has rebelled against God.

Through the Spirit Christians have direct communion with the unseen world. They look at the Scriptures from this perspective and are therefore enabled to catch its whole harmony and deep significance. They also understand the limitations of the Bible, in that it is the revelation of God within the framework of human language.

The story is told that when Robert Moffat, missionary to South Africa, wanted to describe an English train to the local tribesmen, he laid down two iron tracks on the ground, then lined up several ox wagons one after another, and finally hung a large steam kettle around the head of the ox in front. No doubt, when Africans later went to Europe and saw a real train, they must have found Moffat's description ridiculous. But the language of the Africans did not allow him to tell them what a train really was. Similarly, God has to use a vocabulary drawn from earthly experiences in dealing with heavenly and spiritual things, for which there are no adequate words in the human language.

But still, how inspiring and uplifting is this book!

Voltaire wrote that in a hundred years' time the Bible would be an outmoded and forgotten book, to be found only in museums. But a hundred years after he wrote this, his own house was being used by the Bible Society.

The Bible has been translated into 1,300 languages, and millions of copies are sold every year—but who bothers to read Voltaire anymore?

There can be no doubt, as far as natural abilities are concerned, that Plato is far above the apostle John, a humble fisherman, or that Marcus Aurelius is far above Peter as a thinker. But today hardly anyone reads Marcus Aurelius or Plato, whereas after two thousand years the writings of John and Peter are words of life to men all over the world.

Scientists are frequently at variance in their application of known data.

Facts about nature can also be misinterpreted. So too can this holy book be misconstrued or misapplied, but that does not diminish its intrinsic value.

Atheists have written hundreds of pages to refute the Bible, a book virtually unknown to them.

If I make the acquaintance of a man, I don't know the man. I see only his clothes and shoes. Of his body, only the head and hands are visible. If I see him naked, I still don't know him, because his soul remains a mystery. The literal text of the Bible is only an outward vestment. Its allegories are its body, its spiritual truths its soul. The beauty of its mysteries are revealed only to the lovers of God, who are willing to open their eyes and hearts to His divine Spirit. A beautiful landscape is perceived by the anatomical eye and interpreted by the brain. Just so, spiritual things, says Paul, are spiritually discerned and are mediated by the Spirit of God.

18

DOES CHRISTIANITY TEACH SERVILITY TOWARD TYRANNICAL AUTHORITIES?

The words of Jesus, "Render to Caesar the things that are Caesar's," are proof enough for the authors of *The Atheist's Handbook* that he taught servility toward what we would call today a colonial ruler.

Now, first of all, Jesus never said these words to His disciples. He said them to His worst adversaries, the Pharisees. Their whole lives were a mockery of religion. So He told them, "Render to Caesar the things that are Caesar's, and to God the things that are God's" (Mark 12:17). He was sure that by striving to do so, His opponents would soon find out that if they were complacent toward mad rulers (many Roman Caesars were mad), there would be nothing left to give to God.

The disciples of Jesus must have understood well what He meant by these words, which have been so often misused.

If somebody has been dishonest and wishes to make things right with those he has defrauded, he first has to establish as best he can what he owes and then pay it back. Now, what did a Jew owe to Caesar? What does a Christian owe to a godless ruler? Nothing.

Even in Rome, nothing belonged rightfully to Caesar. Julius Caesar, a victorious Roman general, upon his return from a campaign in Gallia overthrew the Republic by military force. He was thus not a legitimate ruler. He was succeeded by tyrants, most of them more fit for an asylum than a throne. These tyrants robbed the population of the Roman Empire of its freedom. They gave nothing to it.

Even less did anything in Palestine belong to Caesar. Profiting from a division between Jewish factions, Guaeus Pompeius occupied by force this small country and imposed upon it a regime of terror and corruption.

Caesar never constructed a road in Palestine. The Jews did the work. He did not build a house. He did not plant a tree. "Render to Caesar what is Caesar's" is a revolutionary, patriotic sentence, which in essence denies any right to the usurper.

If any honest-thinking citizen in the Soviet Union had been told during the Nazi invasion, "Give to Hitler what is Hitler's and to God what is God's," he would have understood those words as meaning, "Give Hitler the boot and throw his troops out, because nothing belongs to him in the Soviet Union. He has no right even to be here." The same would apply to past Soviet invasions in neighboring countries.

The Roman authorities, and the Jewish high priests who were their stooges, evidently gave to the words of Jesus my interpretation. The proof is that they did not consider him a loyal citizen of the empire but a rebel, and they crucified him.

Critics simply misrepresent the truth when they portray the authors of the New Testament as flatterers of the Roman authorities.

"It contains no accusation against the Roman governor," they say. "All the guilt of the crucifixion is attributed to the Jews, while Pilate is described as a passive observer."

It is easy to make such assertions in a country where Bibles are scarce. In Acts 4:27 we read: "For truly in this city there were gathered together against your holy servant Jesus, whom you anointed, both Herod and Pontius Pilate, along with the Gentiles and the peoples of Israel." A Jewish mob, incited by priests, had asked for the crucifixion of Jesus. But Pilate on his own initiative added cruelty to cruelty. We know it from the words, "Then Pilate took Jesus and flogged him" (John 19:1). The text implies the utter debasement of a Roman governor who finds pleasure in personally whipping a prisoner about whose innocence he is obviously convinced. Then the Gospel says very clearly that Pilate delivered Him to be crucified.

John is not the only one to accuse the Roman governor. All the Evangelists reveal him as a henchman. Matthew writes that Pilate, "having scourged Jesus, delivered him to be crucified" (Matthew 27:26). Mark writes, "Pilate, wishing to satisfy the crowd, released for them Barabbas, and having scourged Jesus, he delivered him to be crucified" (Mark 15:15). Luke quotes Pilate explicitly as saying,

"I did not find this man guilty...I will therefore punish and release him" (Luke 23:14,16).

The authors of the New Testament never whitewashed the Romans for their part in the crucifixion of Jesus. They share in the guilt. Later church historians reported with fidelity how Roman authorities threw Christians to the wild beasts and subjected them to all kinds of atrocities.

Far from being servile, as accused, true Christians in all ages have never recognized tyrants as their legitimate rulers. Neither did they consider it a duty to be submissive to them. The first book against Christianity of which we have any knowledge is *The True Word* by Celsus. Its date is around AD 175. It reproaches Christians for not defending the emperor, fighting for him, participating in his military expeditions, or working. Christians should look upon evil leaders as oppressors. They will get no flattery from the disciples of Christ.

Skeptics and even ignorant Christians quote another Scripture to show that Christianity teaches blind submission to unjust rulers and is, therefore, a hindrance to the progress of humanity. The text is Romans 13:1,2: "Let every person be subject to the governing authorities. For there is no authority except from God, and those that exist have been instituted by God. Therefore whoever resists the authorities resists what God has appointed, and those who resist will incur judgment."

But this same chapter defines what a Christian means by the "authority" to whom he owes obedience. Only he deserves this name who, as the minister of God, gives praise to those who do good and executes wrath on the wrongdoer (vv. 3,4). If a ruler does the contrary, if he punishes good and rewards evil, we can no longer recognize his power as being from God.

Bible verses such as the foregoing made Christians resist tyranny.

In the Middle Ages, Savonarola was burned at the stake because he had said, "Nothing is more abhorrent to a tyrant than service to Christ and a virtuous Christian life. For these are diametrically opposed to his own habits."

I quote from a discussion between Mary Queen of Scots and the Protestant Reformer John Knox:

Mary: "Ye have taught the people to receive another religion than their princes can allow. And how can that doctrine be of God, seeing that God commands subjects to obey their princes?"

Knox: "Madame, as right religion neither took original strength nor authority from worldly princes, but from the Eternal God alone, so are not subjects bound to frame their religion according to the appetites of their princes . . . If all the seed of Abraham should have been of the religion of Pharaoh . . . what religion would have been in the world? Or if all the men in the days of the apostles should have been of the religion of the Roman emperors, what religion could there have been on the face of the earth?"

Mary: "Yes, but none of these men raised the sword against their princes."

Knox: "Yet, Madame, ye cannot deny, but that they resisted. For these that obey not . . . in some sort resist."

Mary: "But yet they resisted not by the sword."

Knox: "God, Madame, had not given them the power and the means."

Mary: "Think ye that subjects having power may resist their princes?"

Knox: "If their princes exceed their bounds, Madame... it is no doubt but they may be resisted, even by power. For what if a father should go mad and try to kill his own children? Should they not seize him and take the sword or weapons from him by force? It is even so, Madame, with princes that would murder the children of God that are subject unto them. Their blind zeal is nothing but a very mad frenzy... and therefore to take the sword from them, to bind their hands and cast them in prison till that they be brought to a more sober mind is no disobedience against princes, but just obedience, because that it agreeth with the will of God."

The Bible inspired Lincoln and Wilberforce to fight for the abolition of slavery. Marx in his *Das Kapital* acknowledges the role of the Christian Shaftesbury in introducing laws protecting labor in the United Kingdom. It was a Russian Christian, Count Leo Tolstoy, who denied any authority to the czar. Thomas Jefferson, president of the United States, wrote, "I have sworn upon the altar of God eternal hostility against every form of tyranny over the mind of man"; and "Rebellion against tyrants is obedience towards God."

Emerson wrote: "If you put a chain around the neck of a slave, the other fastens itself around your own."

Lincoln wrote: "If slavery is not wrong, nothing is wrong." In his message to the Congress on December 1, 1862, he said, "In giving freedom to the slaves, we give freedom to the free."

But all these arguments are not really necessary because, as usual, *The Atheist's Handbook* contradicts itself. In order to explain the miraculous growth and victory of Christianity, the atheists, who cannot admit that God was working in the Church, claim that it proselyted mostly slaves "because slaves gained in Christian circles a position which they could not enjoy with others."

In the Epistle to Philemon, Paul urges a slaveowner to receive back one of his servants who had fled, not only without punishment but "as a beloved brother" (Philemon 16). This was the spirit of primitive Christianity.

Why then did the first Christians not abolish slavery? They were persecuted. They had no power in the state. Many of them were slaves themselves. Only a short time before, the great revolt of slaves led by Spartacus had been bloodily suppressed and many tens of thousands of slaves crucified. Only fools rebel when the sure outcome of rebellion is defeat.

God has appeared only once on Mount Sinai, giving the Ten Commandments. The preamble to them is: "I am the LORD your God, who brought you out of the land of Egypt, out of the house of slavery." In introducing Himself to His people, He chooses to characterize Himself as the liberator of slaves, rather than as the Creator of heaven and earth. This is our God.

I was in jail under Stalin and under his successors. Would the underground church of Russia not have more right than the atheists to speak about opposing tyranny?

True Christians have been and are fighters for freedom. In this matter we have nothing to learn from our atheist friends. The United States, Great Britain, and Australia do not have slave labor camps, but the Soviet Union did and China, Vietnam, and other countries still do today.

To describe Christians as a bunch of sycophants to tyrants is only to caricature them. What atheists reject therefore is not Christianity, but a travesty of it.

19

A HEAVENLY OR AN EARTHLY PARADISE

The Atheist's Handbook quotes Friedrich Engels as saying that Christianity's hope is in heaven, in eternal life after death. According to him, Christianity does not have the will to carry out a social transformation in this world.

This is pure fiction.

It is not true that Christianity has only a heavenly goal. Jesus taught us to pray, "Your will be done, on earth as it is in heaven." In John 3:12 He reminds us, "I have told you earthly things…"

In the very beginning of the Gospel of Luke, we are told that when people asked John the Baptist what to do, he did not answer, "Strive for eternal life." The Baptist's answers were very earthly: "Whoever has two tunics is to share with him who has none, and whoever has food is to do likewise." To tax collectors he said, "Collect no more than you are authorized to do." And to soldiers he did not say, "Seek heaven," but rather, "Do not extort money from anyone by threats or by false accusation, and be content with your wages," which were higher than those of the average population (Luke 3:11–14).

Jesus drove merchants out of the temple with a whip. He publicly accused scribes and Pharisees of devouring widows' houses. To a rich young man, He said, "If you would be perfect, go, sell what you possess and give to the poor" (Matthew 19:21).

Christianity has in its program a social transformation in this world, too. The main teaching of the gospel is that a Christian must follow the example of Christ. Was Christ Himself passive toward injustice? How did the merchants driven out with a whip feel about His attitude? Was it passive resistance when He confronted the priests and Pharisees in their own temple, calling them vipers and hypocrites?

Wisdom taught the disciples of Christ to be passive and meek in situations of Christian witness. However, when tyranny has threatened, Christians have justly responded to the call.

When the peasants rebelled against the landlords in the time of the Reformation, the principal arguments in favor of their cause were religious. Their revolutionary hymns were:

> When Adam delved and Eve span,
> Who was then the gentleman?

And

> A mighty fortress is our God,
> A bulwark never failing.

When the movement of the industrial proletariat started in Britain, the song of the Chartists was:

Britannia's sons, though slaves you be,
God your Creator made you free;
To all he life and freedom gave,
But never, never, made a slave.

The first to organize the demonstration that led to the revolution of 1905 in Russia were not the Communists, but Christian workers under the leadership of a priest, Gapon. The Communists profited from it and later hanged the priest.

Christianity is as revolutionary as was communism, but our revolutions differ. Communist revolutions were always negative and destructive.

We Christians are revolutionary in an entirely different sense. Christians use first and foremost the sword of the Spirit, which can kill sin without killing the sinner.

By the sword of the Spirit, Christians have corrected many abuses. Where Christian civilization reigns, men are free, free even to be atheists. I defy my honored opponents to give me the name of a single man who is in prison in the United States, Great Britain, or West Germany for being an atheist. But in former Communist countries millions of my brethren and sisters in faith have passed through jails or have been killed. Who has fought for freedom and obtained it—atheists or Christians?

Christians do not exclude the necessity of rebellion against tyranny. When oppressors by their excesses force them to rebel and the circumstances are favorable, their aim is always to replace tyranny with a regime favoring peace and justice, whereas Marx advocated "permanent revolution," an expression he created. Permanent revolution for what? Revolution for revolution's sake? Never a goal to be reached? Never even a Utopia to aim for? This is sheer sadism.

Christians never forget that the first rebel was the devil. They do not resort to rebellion easily, not even to rebellion against the Communist regime.

But they are interested in earthly destinies, only that they have more than earthly aims. Men are like frogs living at the bottom of some dark well, from which they can see nothing of the outside world. Believers are men who, while living in such conditions, have heard the singing of a skylark. And miracle of miracles—they have understood the song! It speaks about sun and moon and stars and tree-covered mountains and hills and a wonderful sea. They have faith in this song. They have the assurance that there exists a heavenly paradise. Without neglecting their earthly duties, they strive toward it and call others to join them.

The Christian believes in a new birth. He believes that a frog can become a lark, that a human being can become a partaker of the divine nature, and this not by a long process, but instantly by faith in Jesus Christ.

Believing all this, Christians fight for justice in this world while striving after the heavenly paradise.

20

IS THERE A GOD?

Until now I have followed in the present book the precept of Jesus: "If anyone forces you to go one mile, go with him two miles."

My opponents wanted to pursue a certain course of arguments. I have walked along with them. I have discussed their arguments even when the issues were not at all important.

But now I would rather concentrate on the principal question at issue between atheists and Christians: Is there a God to worship, to rely upon, to be protected by, to be comforted with, or not?

According to the French atheist theoretician R. Garaudy, totality and absoluteness is not God, but "the name man." There is nothing superior to man. Christians believe in God and in His promises to assist them in this life and to provide life eternal. Garaudy writes, "To us atheists, nothing is promised and nobody waits for us." Sad words indeed! To atheists, not even the loyal friendship of their own comrades is promised. Garaudy was rejected by his atheist friends. Nobody waited to extend him a helping hand or a friendly gesture when he was in distress. He found himself alone.

A young composer was poor and had to live in a rented room. A friend encouraged him, "When you die, there will be an inscription on the wall of this house." The composer was enthusiastic, "You really mean it?" "Surely," was the reply. "There will be an inscription ROOM TO RENT." No more than this can Garaudy wait for after death.

Man is God. The whole atheist-humanist creed breathes this belief.

Having in view this delusion, one of the Soviet underground poets, I. Gabai, was moved to write the following verses:

Late Credo of Job

I'm my own god. But what a weak, erratic god,
Irrational, insane, and feeble.
May God forbid that one love such a god
And be like him—may God protect you from it!

A god?—perhaps. A vicious, wretched god.
But if indeed I am the "Guileless Face,"
May God help you to be a peaceful atheist;
To be a god—from that may God protect you.

A god I am—but pow'rless in the tumult.
And by the logic of perverted borders,
Museums are now dwelling in the temples,
And gods are living in the midst of milling crowds.

Forgive me for my mania of grandeur,
But there is no God's greatness in my fate
Myself to punish and forgive myself my sins.
Forgive my mania of grandeur!

God's greatness—to chastise—
I would not wish to any of my neighbors,
I do not dare to wish him such command.
May God forbid that you should stoop to godhead,
To exculpate yourself or to absolve yourself from sin.

I'm what I am. God—only He is God.
What an enormous pride, what sorrow;
May God forbid that you should trust your conscience
And live defying it. May God forbid!

Is there a Being superior to man? Is there a God, in the usual sense given to this word, the Creator of heaven and earth, the One whom Jesus taught us to call our Father?

In the temple of Jerusalem (as well as in many Egyptian and Mithraist temples), there was a most holy place in which only the high priest was allowed to enter once a year, in the framework of an impressive religious ceremony.

In the time of Jesus, this most holy place was empty. The so-called ark of the covenant, a gilded case containing tables of stone with the Commandments of God, had been carried away and hidden centuries before by Jeremiah at the time of the Babylonian captivity. When the temple was reconstructed after the release of the Jews from captivity, the sacred ark could not be found. There was absolutely nothing in the most holy place.

This emptiness had a symbolic significance.

The Kabala, an esoteric book of the Jews which contains their ancient religious traditions, calls God *"Ein"*—the nonexistent. It might seem strange to find in a deeply religious book a name of God with which atheists would agree. But the sense is clear for those who know God.

"God is not" in the sense that "He is not what we consider Him to be." His thoughts are not our thoughts, and His ways are not our ways.

Feuerbach was right when he said that men have created gods according to their own image. But Feuerbach was not original. He said this in order to deprecate God. Luther, one of the profoundest religious thinkers of history, had said three centuries before, *"Fides creatrix divinitatis"* (Faith is the creator of God).

Man thinks about the causes and purposes of things, about the mysteries of nature and of life, and his mind gives birth to the notion of God. God is his son, the beloved child of his thought. But once he comes to this point, he immediately concludes that this God born in his mind is the Creator of all things and also of his own person, that He has an objective existence outside his own consciousness, that man owes Him everything. So from God the Son, he arrives at the notion of God the Father. These two notions, we learn from the Bible, are united with each other in an ineffable, unspeakable love, the Holy Spirit. God created the man who has faith. Faith creates the notion "God."

Thus far we understand our notion of God.

But the God who created us far surpasses our understanding. He is not what our reason can conceive.

Theology has given many arguments that God exists. To this, adversaries of religion have brought counter-arguments.

I will not argue. Woe to a God who needs somebody to defend Him. A God can reveal Himself. You need bring no proof for the existence of the sun—how much less then for its Creator. There are moments when the sun is veiled by clouds. Then those who wish to see it have to wait. If God wishes to hide Himself so as to be discovered only by those who seek Him zealously, I have to respect His will.

God uses light to give life to every being, but both God and light are unseen. Who has ever seen light? In a tube completely empty of air, a ray of light remains invisible. What we call seeing light is seeing the objects, the air illuminated by light. Light as such is invisible.

So one has to override the senses and reason in order to know God, though reason may point toward Him.

You observe purposes in nature. The seed sown in the earth extracts from its surroundings just as much nitrogen, air, and water as it needs in order to become a flower. You can see a finality in its growth. It has a purpose to attain. The impregnated egg takes from the womb of the mother just the food it needs to become a baby. Again the reaching toward a goal. But neither the seed nor the egg can pursue aims. These must come from a wise Being who imposes them upon His creations.

Furthermore, we see man attuned to his environment, or he could not have survived so many thousands of years. That is, in spite of man's abuses, we live in a reality which, sometimes with and sometimes without our effort, gives us what is necessary for our existence. We are born as babes able to consume nothing but milk, and a short time before our birth, milk accumulates in our mother's breasts.

We are born with lungs and we find air. We need water and it is provided. After several months we need the nutrients found in vegetables and meat and the world contains these.

We are susceptible to sickness. But we know now that someone has prepared medicines for innumerable kinds of sickness from herbs or other plants.

For every human need there is a corresponding reality to supply that need.

What arrogance or ignorance makes us suppose that for a very fundamental need, for the thirst of our soul after a God—a thirst which has created so many mythologies and religions—there should be no fulfilling reality?

One autumn day a crow spoke with a young swallow in its first year of life. The crow said to the swallow, "I see you are preparing for a long journey. Where are you flying?" The swallow answered, "It is growing colder and colder here. I might freeze. I fly toward a warmer country." The wise crow mocked, "But remember well your birth. You were born here only a couple of months ago. How do you know that there is a warmer country to shelter you while it is cold here?" The swallow answered, "The One who has put in my heart the desire for a warm climate cannot have cheated me. I believe Him and depart." And the swallow found what it sought.

That is how every faithful soul proceeds.

The human soul becomes an icicle in a world without God. You remember Homunculus—the artificial man created in a tube in the second part of *Faust*. He always felt cold. You freeze when you think of yourself as only a complicated product of chemical reactions. We aspire toward a Father, source of warmth, love, light. As all fundamental human needs are fulfilled in reality, so also is this need of the soul. We can find God. We can know Him.

However, no field of knowledge can be investigated without proper tools. You cannot see stars through the microscope or microbes through the telescope. Men who cannot think rightly come to the conclusion that God does not exist because they cannot find Him through the senses, which are functions of life in the realm of matter. Senses are not the right means to see God.

As microbiology has its particular instrument and astronomy another, faith also possesses one by which it can see the Creator. Jesus said, "Blessed are the pure in heart, for they shall see God" (Matthew 5:8). Have such a heart, and you will see!

The reader will surely understand that the word "to see" has many meanings. I see a material object because the photons reflected by it hit my eye. I see the righteousness of a cause by weighing arguments in my mind. I see the love of a person toward me by his behavior. I close my eyes and can evoke the image of someone dear. He is far away. No photons from him reach my eye. But I see. I can tell my dream, my daydream, my fancies. Half of our lives, we see in this manner.

How do we see God?

In our imagination are stored images, and we can pick up the image we need as if from an album. But it is not only images from the material world that we have in this safe. My existence does not start on the day of my birth, nor on the day of my conception. I have existed forever in the mind and plan of God. I have come on this earth for a short time as a pilgrim and foreigner.

But we have to qualify the words "to see" and "image" in this connection, because you see a reality for which there are no words in human language.

When Marco Polo, the first European ever to be in China, returned and told his fellows that he had met men with slanted eyes and with hair tressed in tails, he was called "Marco Polo, the liar." What means did he have to prove his assertions? He could only say to men, "Go where I have been, face the dangers I have faced, bear with the fatigues through which I passed, and you will know."

I cannot convince a skeptic that viruses exist. He himself has to look in a microscope.

Blessed are the pure in heart, because they will see God. The problem of knowing God is one of purity of character. The ultimate truth is the exclusive monopoly of the clean. Whenever somebody speaks to me about God, for or against, I ask him, "How pure are you that you may be considered reliable? Only those can know this subject who are whiter than snow."

21

WHO IS GOD?

Since atheists do not accept the sacrifice of Christ on the cross which cleanses us from sin, they cannot see God. But they are right to say to us, "You assert that you see God. Tell us who He is!"

A very important question! It exists for both sides. Atheists must be able to say, "Who is the one whose existence we deny?", just as Christians must give an answer to the question, "Who is the One in whom we believe?"

Who is God?

De Broglie, the greatest contemporary theoretician in problems of light, wrote, "How much we would know if we knew what a ray of light is." The great biologist Jacob von Uexkull wrote, "No one of us knows what life is." And we are asked to answer who the Giver of life and light is!

Where is the difficulty in answering? When you ask, "What is light or life?" or "Who is God?" the difficulty lies not in the words "What," "Who," "life," "light," or "God." Somehow we can say what we mean by these words. What spoils the intelligibility is the smallest word in the questioning proposition: the word "is." What does the word "is" mean? If we do not understand this, all the rest remains enigmatic.

A great division passes through Christianity. It centers around the word "is." According to the New Testament, which was actually written in Greek, at His last supper with the disciples before the crucifixion, Jesus had given them bread, saying, "This is my body," and a cup of wine, saying, "This is my blood" (Matthew 26:26,28). Orthodox and Catholic Christians believe that the word "is" in this context can mean only one thing: that Christians eat and drink at communion the real body and blood of Jesus. When the priests repeat the words of Jesus during the liturgy, a change takes place in the elements. Outwardly, they remain bread and wine. But the essence has been transformed. What were bread and wine have become the body of Christ. Protestants read the same Bible and interpret the word "is" otherwise. It means for them that the bread at communion symbolizes the body of Christ, that whereas it is still only bread, it has another value, just as a ring has increased value for the receiver when it comes from the beloved.

The fact that thousands of books have been written on this subject and great institutions split apart shows that the word "is" is not as simple as it looks. You who wish to know "Who is God?" or "What is light?" must first tell me what you understand by "is."

Christianity was not negative toward previous cultures. As we have said already, it incorporated in its thinking Greek philosophy, predominantly from Aristotle. Christianity took the concept of a God who, Himself unmovable, produces all the movement in the world. He sits quietly on an unshaken throne and rules all things and men in their unceasing motion. Aristotle would have said that God "is" in the very strict sense of the word.

But an unmoved mover is inconceivable. What is static cannot be active. A motor which moves a machine has its own movements. To a motor another notion applies beyond mere being—it moves.

Reality does not know a being. Kant wrote in *Critic of Pure Reason*, "*To be* is no real predicate... In logical usage it is only the copula or link of a judgment." To say that God is good or righteous makes sense. To say that God or any other subject simply is, means to remain in the realm of vain words.

When we ask ourselves what Being means, the answer is that being exists only as a becoming, an evolving, a moving, a being changed. Heraclitus said, *"Panta rhei"*—"Everything flows." You cannot bathe twice in the same stream. "You" cannot bathe in it even "once," because in this one period while you bathe, your body is changing, and the river too.

The elementary particles of which the world is composed, the chemical elements, as well as the spiritual realities, are not existences, but events, happenings. While I pronounce the word "iron," the electrons in the atoms of iron will have revolved many billions of times around the nucleus. When I come to the last letter "n," the iron is no longer in the same state as it was when I pronounced the first letter "i." Descend into the realm of microphysics and you will see the importance of apprehending this. No elementary particle in its continual motion has patience enough to stay in its place at least long enough to give me time to say about it that "it is." While I say "The atom is," it has lived a history so rich that in comparison to it the whole history of mankind appears as a little thing. Sir James Jeans said, "Matter is not something which is, but which happens." Matter is not existence, but flowing. Everything —and especially living beings—is continually changing and being renewed.

How can the One who moves everything be unmoved? If images of God were allowed and could convey reality, the most faithful image of God would be that painted by Michelangelo on the ceiling of the Sistine chapel, which shows God flying in the tempest. In the biblical Book of Ruth, we read about the wings of God.

My opponents say that God is not. They don't know that high-ranking Christian teachers said it long before, though they gave this negation the right meaning. The scholastic philosopher John Scotus Erigena wrote, "Literally, God is not, because he transcends being." Thomas Aquinas says, "The divine 'being,' which is his substance, is not the common 'to be.' It is a being distinct from any other being. The divine 'Esse' (Latin: to be) is not the common 'esse.'"

The word "being" is not only a noun, but also a verb. No created being is something which could be expressed only by a noun, because it evolves, it moves, it lives a history. You cannot apply the category "is" in the limited sense of having a fixed state to the creation, even less to the Creator. When you say "God is," you have said much too little about Him. God happens.

There exists an event, "Godhead." He is a huge coming and becoming. His name in Hebrew is *El*, which expresses a relation: "El" means "toward," the movement from Alpha toward Omega.

The literal translation of His Hebrew name which He disclosed to Moses, *Ehjeh asher ehjeh*, is "I will be what I will be."

David the psalmist asked himself who God was and answered, "He rode on a cherub [an angelic being] and flew; he came swiftly on the wings of the wind" (Psalm 18:10). The Bible tells us that God rides on winged beings, or rather on winged events, because the angels also "are" not, but happen. In another psalm we read of God who "makes the clouds his chariot; he rides on the wings of the wind" (104:3).

Compare this imagery, which is a genial anticipation of the modern scientific conception of the world, with the idea of an immobile motor of the universe and you will discover how right the Bible is. In God there is no variableness, nor shadow of turning, as regards His fixed character of love. But the manifestations of this love are new every moment.

This creates the difficulty in answering the question "Who is God?" because He sheds His goodness upon mankind in ever new forms. The flames of His love are changing continually, as do flames of fire. You cannot really make a portrait of a person. Every person is a succession of many facial expressions. You cannot really say a truth. Truth is always a whole chain of assertions about a changing object or person.

Therefore Hebrew, the language in which God first gave His revelation, does not have the word "face," but only "faces"—*panim*. Every man and every object changes its aspect continually. About God Himself the Bible also uses this plural, *panim*. He also changes constantly His expressions of love and righteousness.

When you ask yourself "Who is God?," thousands of images pass like in a kaleidoscope before your eyes, each more beautiful than the other. Therefore it was forbidden to the Jews to make to themselves graven images.

The Hebrew language avoids the expression "is." Jesus, speaking Hebrew or its Aramaic dialect, never said, "This is my body" but simply, "This—my body." (Russians, as well as the Chinese, also omit the verb "to be.") If theologians had known the biblical languages better, there would have been one quarrel less about what Jesus never said.

We know what God is: the Alpha, the Creator of heaven and earth. We know what He will be: the "all in all." What is He now? He is not an "is."

The atheists have a point. We cannot say who God is, nor can they say what atheism is. This also is in continual evolution. The atheism of the fools of old who simply denied God has passed through many stages to become the militant and scientifically substructed atheism ruling in Communist countries today.

But the fact that we cannot say who God is does not exhaust our thinking.

The apostle Paul wrote, "For his invisible attributes, namely, his eternal power and divine nature, have been clearly perceived, ever since the creation of the world, in the things that have been made" (Romans 1:20).

Giordano Bruno is the author of the play on words that *intelectio* (the intellect) is *interna lectio* (the internal lesson) which nature gives us.

The more I know of a machine, the more I admire the engineer who conceived it. The more beautiful a palace, the more respect I have for the architect.

The list of atheist scientists given by my opponents is spurious.

Our universe bears the name of Einstein. He must know something about it. He writes in *The World As I See It:*

If one purges the Judaism of the prophets, and Christianity as Jesus Christ has taught it, of all subsequent additions, specially of priestcraft, one is left with a teaching which is capable of curing all the social evils of humanity. It is the duty of every man of good will to strive steadfastly in his own little world to make this really human teaching a living force, as far as he can. If he makes an honest effort in this direction, without being crushed and trampled under feet by his contemporaries, he may consider himself and the community to which he belongs lucky.

In a preface to his biography by Bernett, he says: "The cosmic living of religion is the most powerful and noble motive for the scientific research of nature."

Milner opens his book *Relativity and the Structure of Stars* with the words: "In the beginning God created heaven and earth."

Immanuel Kant wrote: "As a face is beautiful because it unveils a soul, the world is beautiful because you see through it a God."

Hegel, the founder of modern dialectic and the teacher of Karl Marx, asked philosophy to save religion.

Francis Bacon said: "Philosophy studied superficially estranges from God: studied in depth it brings you back to God."

There are many things which make believers of many scientists. They wonder about the concordance between the laws of nature and our possibilities of apprehension through the senses, reason, intuition, and faith.

Unbelievers, if they wish to be logical, should not be atheists but agnostics. Is there no Creator? Well, then, the universe is the random agglomeration, unguided by any wisdom, of ions, electrons, photons, and protons. My brain is also the result of such random evolution, according to the laws established by no lawgiver. How is it, then, that my brain, which is not a willed organ, intelligently constructed, can rightly understand so many things in the universe? Stalin said that not all things are known, but all things can be known. How is it that I have a brain which can know everything? Would lamps, batteries, and wires thrown together without a preconceived design be able to catch radio transmissions? Would wheels, screws, levers, and brakes come together to make a car in which one can drive?

The biologist Max Hartmann speaks about "the miracle of the harmony between the universe and our thinking." De Broglie says that there is more mystery than we believe in the simple fact that science is possible. Einstein wrote: "What is eternally unintelligible in the universe is that it can be understood."

Even Voltaire, whom the atheists wrongly consider to be one of their number, said these words: "The world is made with intelligence. Therefore it has been made by an intelligence... The intelligence of a Newton comes from another intelligence."

Who can believe that there are watches but no watchmakers? Our watches tell time according to the movements of the earth. Who made this chronometer?

The second thing which strikes everyone who looks attentively at creation is the stern order in nature, which also cannot be the result of chance.

Uexkull says: "We read in nature a whole musical score." The geologist Cloos writes: "We hear the music of the earth."

Kant, who is very critical of many reasonable proofs brought by theology for belief in the existence of God, admits the validity of the so-called cosmological proof. The order in nature points to a Creator.

Charles Darwin, victim of the mercantilist and utilitarian style of life in Great Britain of his time, thought nature also worked according to the utilitarian principle. But this is not so. In nature a great Artist and Architect with imagination is at work.

The exquisite beauty of the peacock's feathers cannot be explained as having evolved by the accumulation of small variations, because they provided the advantage of more easily attracting mates. A female crow also finds a mate, and wayside weeds as well as gorgeous lilies attract bees and wasps for fertilization.

Why are some tiny fish so uselessly beautiful? Well, it is art for art's sake. Why does the parrot have the capacity to speak? Why do bellbirds exist, whose chirping is like the ringing of little bells? It is just the fancy of an artist. How about the horns of the deer? Why does the zebra have such regular stripes? Why does each flower have a different color?

Nietzsche said: "In every one of us there is a child who wishes to play." Is there not something childlike in God which made Him create all these things? Does it not belong to the very essence of

Godhead that it must be expressed also in a Babe born in a stable and in a little Boy who plays with others on the streets of Nazareth?

From where came the precise angles and the symmetry and beauty of forms in crystals?

How is it that in the Far East there exists the tailorbird, which sows its nest of leaves with threads of cotton spun by itself?

How is it that the spiderweb surpasses the technical capacities of men? On astronomical lenses the thread of the spiderweb is used for measure. Men could not produce anything better or finer which would last longer and not be altered by changes of temperature.

Men have invented radar. But they learned it from the bats. We have wonderful optical instruments today, but which one surpasses the human eye?

I know about a Communist who became a Christian from looking at the delicate convolutions of his baby's ears. They were surely created by design. They could not have been created by any chance coming together of atoms.

How can you not believe in a wise Creator when you investigate further the human ear, in which 24,000 nerve ends are united and strung in order to bring messages to the brain?

Look carefully at a stalk of wheat: its height would be something like four and a half feet and the diameter would be a mere sixteenth of an inch. For comparison let us imagine a building 1,250 feet high. (It would be a building of something like 100 stories). And this on a surface of only one square yard. Now, just at the top of the stalk is the heavy fruit. It is moved by winds but does not break. The stalk contains a splendidly conceived mechanical system. It is still a mystery to men how the water ascends to the very top. We need pumps to provide water for the upper floors of our high buildings. We could not make something as marvelous as the stalk.

The physicist Urey, the discoverer of heavy water (used in Norwegian research for the atomic bomb), wrote: "Not one of the existing theories about the origin of the world does work without the presupposition of a miracle."

And because we spoke about water—let us stop to look at its wonders. All physical objects expand with heat and contract with cold; only water increases its volume when it cools down and forms ice. The ice, being lighter than water, remains on top. It forms a crust, which saves the fish from the cold of winter. Without this peculiarity of water, life in the rivers would be impossible, and animals that lived on fish would not have survived.

What is the origin of this exception? Is it just an accident, or is it something ordered by a wise Creator?

Let us allow a renowned technician, Verner Siemens, to speak:

> The more we penetrate in the sphere of the harmonic forces of nature, which are regulated by eternal, immovable laws, hidden from our full understanding by a thick veil, the more we are pushed towards humility, the more our knowledge appears small, the more our desire to drink from this unquenchable source of science and

knowledge increases. And in the same measure also grows our admiration towards the infinite ordering wisdom, which is interpenetrating the whole creation.

It is true that we cannot say, "Who is God?" but His unseen power can be seen if we look carefully at the things created by Him. They speak about God as a mighty Ruler and a great Artist. From them we know that God is a God of order.

Jesus, asked once by His disciples to show them the Father, answered, "Have I been with you so long, and you still do not know me, Philip? Whoever has seen me has seen the Father. How can you say, 'Show us the Father'? Do you not believe that I am in the Father and the Father is in me? . . . The Father who dwells in me does his works" (John 14:9,10).

By these words, Jesus teaches us how we should think about His person, but He also teaches us how we should think about ourselves.

While maintaining a sense of proportion, let us note that whoever sees me or whoever sees you, even if you are the author of an atheistic book, sees the Father, because we were all created in His image and after His likeness.

Gregory of Nyssa wrote, "Man is the human face of God." Macarius wrote, "Between God and man there exists the closest familial relationship."

Man, every man, any man—an atheist, a criminal, a saint—is wonderful first of all because of his bodily structure. Even the worst and most despicable of men has a heart, which is a pump such as engineers are not able to construct—a pump which circulates the blood 600 times a day throughout the body. In a span of fifty years, this happens 1,840,000,000 times, and without a single minute of interruption.

Secondly, man is a wonderful creature by virtue of his soul, another surprising entity, almost indefinable. It is so perfect that, in a certain sense, it can dispense with the body. It shows its independence in the Ninth Symphony of the deaf Beethoven; or in the dedicated life of Helen Keller, who, though deaf, dumb, and blind, became an author and a great philanthropist; or in the fact that Pascal at the age of nine rediscovered the axioms of Euclidian geometry; or in the life of Mozart, who began composing music at the age of five.

It also shows its independence from the senses in the experiences of clairvoyance, telepathy, precognition, and hypnotism.

In the hypnotic state the beating of the heart becomes so slight that it is almost like fibrillation. The man scarcely breathes at all. The blood barely moves through the vessels of the brain. It might not reach the capillary vessels. Without proper oxygenation, it is clogged with the products of decomposition. The brain engages in a minimum of activity, but the mind of the hypnotized person becomes hyperactive. It is enough to read a long poem to him once. He will repeat it without a mistake. Read to him a page of the Hebrew Bible. He may not know the language, but he will echo it with exactitude. He will recall insignificant incidents from childhood.

So much lies within the province of the soul.

But man contains a third wonderful structure. If by his body he is akin to the animal world (this is nothing to be ashamed of, even if one is scientifically opposed to the theory of evolution. Francis of Assisi spoke about "brother wolf" and would gladly have said "brother monkey"), he has also a spirit, by which he is akin to God.

My adversaries would not even acknowledge its existence, because it cannot be verified by the senses. How can it when it is the verifier? The eye does not see itself, the nose does not smell itself. The spirit does not belong to the spectacle acted upon by the senses. It is the spectator and reacts according to its own taste to what comes within its purview.

Aristotle said, "If you recognize in man only the human, you betray man and wish him mischief, because by everything which is essential in his being—the spirit—man is called to something higher than just human life." It is inhuman to be only human. It is unworthy of a caterpillar to be considered only a caterpillar—he is also a butterfly in process. So we are not allowed to degrade man, who bears the image of God. In a seed there is more than the seed; it contains the potential flower.

I cannot tell you what God looks like, but look to man, look at the best exemplars of mankind, and you will see something of the Godhead. You will see the joy of living, of creative enthusiasm, the depths of knowledge, the taste for beauty, the exuberance of life, and the sheer ability to discern possibilities and choose to reach ever higher.

What a great being man is! He is in the likeness and image of God, because he is also the creator of a universe, of his own inner universe. Nature outside of me is a seething maelstrom of energy, a multitude of waves, radiations, and vibrations of electrons, protons, and elementary particles; but the wave which is dumb becomes audible in an ear, the unapprehended radiation becomes visible in an eye, and the unintelligible universe becomes intelligible in the mind of a man.

Outside of me, there exists a reality. I order it in quantity, quality, causality, finality, modality. I catch this seemingly chaotic reality in a net, which has been woven by me, and make out of it an ordered universe. It is in me that nature realizes its own beauty. When I look upon a rose, it comes to life in crimson splendor and yields its fragrance. If man did not exist, the rose would have no value and would be a mere congregation of atoms.

The only subject in nature which I know intimately from the inside is myself. And in myself there is the capacity to put order in chaos, to create my own universe—whether benevolent, to give me joy, or gloomy, to drive me and others to despair. In all spheres of knowledge we live by extrapolation. We proceed from the known to the unknown. If I myself am more than any outside observer can see, is it not possible that there is more to the world around me than what appears on the surface?

Lenin compliments Bishop Berkeley, the founder of Solipsist philosophy, by calling him the ideal philosopher most difficult to defeat, all because Berkeley provided a reasonable argument for faith in God, an argument which seems very powerful to me. He says that the universe can exist only in a mind; outside the mind reality is chaotic. It is a *tohu va bohu*. It is the mind which organizes from it a universe, dictating its laws, putting it in the frame of order, and categorizing it. A universe can exist only in a mind; but men have not existed forever, nor has the human mind. Therefore, before the appearance of man, there must have been another mind in which the universe existed. Man conceives of himself as part of an organized universe. The mind in which the universe always existed is called God.

I am also a creator of a universe, of an inner universe—but I *am* a creator! Therefore, whosoever sees me, sees the Father.

I cannot tell you who God is, but you can understand something about the Godhead by looking at man.

22

LOOK TO JESUS OF NAZARETH

Look to the highest and best exemplar of mankind that you know, to the most beloved being, and you will see in him, however dimly, something of the Father!

But there is a Son of man in whom you can see God in a special way. It is Jesus of Nazareth—because He was not only the Son of man, He was God incarnate.

God knows everything, but there are some things which He knew only from outside. A judge can know the whole penal code, the whole science of penitentiaries, and still not be able to judge righteously, because he has never lived the life of a prisoner. Five years of prison, lived day by day in a jail, are something entirely different from five years of prison prescribed for an offense in the penal code and pronounced in a sentence.

God cannot lie, nor does He know by experience any other infractions of the moral code, whereas these sins are the very elements of life with which you are surrounded every day. Neither

God nor holy angels can die. Death is for them only a spectacle on which they look from outside.

Therefore Christ, the Son of God, became man with all the attributes and limitations of the human family. A male being, He knew the temptation of woman; a poor carpenter in an oppressed nation, He knew the temptation of rebellion or of dishonesty. A prisoner who was whipped and then crucified, He knew the temptation of despair and resentment. He knew, without committing sin, such depths of evil that the Evangelists considered it wise not to record what happened in His life between the ages of twelve and thirty. But they did record that, during His three and a half years of public ministry, His enemies were frequently offended by His friendship with scoundrels and loose women.

Jesus, the Son of God, chose to partake of human nature with all its liabilities and to taste of death, thus enabling Himself to be not only the righteous judge of man, but also his defender and Savior. The life of Jesus and His death on Golgotha's cross— apart from its efficacy in the salvation of man—was God's way of obtaining a personal, intimate knowledge of human problems. And now, having identified with us in the flesh, He understands us better and can forgive us better. The kingdom of heaven has come closer to us.

To what could we compare this great condescension of the Son of God?

We could liken it to the attempt on the part of Osborn to better the harsh conditions in U.S. prisons by having himself jailed and living for many years the tortured life of a prisoner—all to prepare himself for his valiant crusade afterward.

We could liken it to the deeds of some doctors who have injected themselves with virulent microbes in order to help their fellowmen through the experiences thus gained.

But no! These likenesses do not tell us anything, because in these cases one man risked his life for other men, his fellow creatures, whereas for Jesus Christ it was entirely different.

Christ is God, and in His sight our world is microscopic. All the nations are before Him as a drop of water in a bucket and as a bit of dust on a scale. His great deed can be likened, rather, to the absurdity of love which a man should have for ill-smelling, blood-sucking insects. They tremble between the fingers of the man who wishes to kill them. But He would become a bug, live the life of a bug with its propensity to harm men, and die the death of a bug. He does this in order that, having regained His former estate, in the end He might be a just judge of insects, protect them from their ruthless exterminators, defend them with authority, and make of them harmless benefactors.

I know that this example will offend many, but it must have seemed incomprehensible to angels that Christ should choose to be incarnate in an ugly, loathsome, and sinful species.

Christ descended not merely to the level of man. In the body of the young virgin Mary, through a process of fertilization which remains ever a mystery, He was reduced to a mere embryo, and passed nine months *in utero* to become a babe, then a youth, then a man. And what kind of Man! He was incarnate not in a hero like Bar Kochbah, not in a great initiate like Appollonius of Tyana, not in a philosopher like Plato. In order to save man, every man, Christ had to be immersed in matter as deeply as mankind is drowned. Therefore, after subjecting Himself to the normal processes of human development, He became a Jewish carpenter, a member of a social class without culture. He had a poor language; He sometimes had to engage in discussions on a humiliating level, because this was the level of the men with whom He debated. He knew weakness, anger, hurt, fear, and He was put in a class with criminals.

Those things in Jesus Christ which are offensive to men become, to those who understand, added incentives to adore His magnificent humility and unfathomable love.

And if you ask Christ why He brought this sacrifice, He answers with majestic simplicity that God so loved the world that He gave His only begotten Son, that whoever believes in Him should not perish, but have everlasting life. He says that the Father sent Him.

We cannot say what God is, but looking to Christ, we understand something of His character. We see that what expresses God best is love, righteousness, and lovingkindness toward mankind. We perceive that He has such love and that this love made Him give His Son to die for us.

23

THE CREATION

But why this detour? Why must we see God in nature, in man, in Christ Jesus? Why can we not see Him face to face?

In the Babylonian Talmud it is said that a heathen emperor demanded of a rabbi, "Show me God!" The rabbi answered, "You will see Him with your eyes on one condition. First, you must look five minutes into the sun." The emperor looked at the sun but immediately had to lower his eyes. Then the rabbi told him, "You cannot look for one minute at the sun, which is an insignificant creation of God—and yet you wish to see the One who gives the stars their brilliance!"

Evidently, for a modern intellectual, faith has its difficulties.

He sees that in the world everything happens according to natural laws. From one thing, another develops according to precise laws, as the things which exist are the result of a former development. Mountains and valleys and rivers and living beings are not creations in the usual sense of this word, as stars are not creations but developments from some former state. Some stars are old, ready to be extinguished, others are in full maturity, others are baby stars. Stars of all ages coexist in the universe. Then—when did the creation take place? The number of species which have disappeared is estimated at half a million. The species which exist now may not always have existed. It is known that there is variation within species (microevolution). In this context, not every living being is a direct creation of God.

The difficulty disappears when we consider God not simply as a Being who has created a world. He is a living and a life-giving God. He moves everything continually according to physical laws, which are expressions of His fixed character. Therefore, it is so difficult to apprehend Him.

Heraclitus said, "It pleases nature to hide itself." This is even truer about God, of whom Solomon says, "The LORD has said that he would dwell in thick darkness" (1 Kings 8:12).

The finer a being is, the more it sheds blessings, itself remaining in the shadow. So is God, and therefore He remains unobserved. We have to seek the source of our blessings. Luther says, "Nothing is small without God being even smaller, nothing is big without God being even bigger, nothing is short without God being even shorter, nothing is long without God being even longer, nothing is wide without God being even wider, nothing is narrow without God being even narrower." Elsewhere in his writings he adds, "Nothing can be more present a Being and more central than God and his might."

And we do not observe God except when His Spirit moves, as we do not observe the air except when the wind blows.

It is only through a spiritual rebirth which faith in the sacrifice of Jesus Christ gives you, that in you are awakened the senses of the spirit, and you feel the presence of the Lord. "Blessed are the pure in heart, for they shall see God," says Jesus (Matthew 5:8).

You see, you do know God, though you cannot say to those who are not pure how He is, because you yourself are no more. You are changed from glory to glory, into His likeness.

24

GOD IS

I have seen Christians dying in jail whose last words were, "God is." Were these wrong? Surely not. I would also like to die with this last assertion on my lips.

We live lives on different levels. A scientist knows that all material objects are whirlwinds of elementary particles, as distant from each other as the earth is from the sun. But he has no hesitation in sitting down on a chair, knowing that it is a very solid object. In one sense, every wall is a huge void within which electrons whirl in vast orbits. But considered on another level, a wall is anything but a void. You have to be careful about this inoffensive wall. You may bump your head very badly if you walk toward it with the atomic theory in your mind.

The same is true of religion. There exists a high, philosophic level where, as we explained, you cannot apply to God the words "to exist" or "to be," because these are too simple. He is more than existing. We Christians have room in our minds to consider the atheistic denial of God. But atheists know reality only as it appears on one level, and therefore they know it falsely, thereby placing themselves in deadly danger. There is another plane on which God simply exists and is.

A partial truth is a dangerous thing. It is not without reason that we value "the truth, the whole truth, and nothing but the truth."

Every cultured man knows that we live simultaneously in the Newtonian and in the Einsteinian universe, each with its own laws. Those who know only the Newtonian universe would not be able to fly to the moon nor have atomic energy. We live simultaneously in a world in which we may not meet God and in a second world, which atheists do not know, in which God simply exists, is, and allows us to hold communion with Him.

It is the world of the spirit, of practical religion.

Chairs and walls and bread exist and are used as such in spite of molecular and atomic theories. Likewise, God simply exists.

On occasion, His presence breaks through self-conscious barriers, especially in moments of crisis.

There are instances known from history, and I have personally known many such cases, of atheists—yes, of Communist leaders —who died in Communist prisons, victims of Party purges, and who in their last moment cried, "God, God!" or "Jesus!"

It would be profitable to ask where this belief in God comes from in the minds of millions of men throughout history. The atheists who deny God deny a notion that exists in their own mind. The English philosopher Locke has predicated the idea that there is nothing in our intellect except what has passed through our senses. A wild man in the jungle of New Guinea would not have in his mind the notion of "television," because the respective object does not exist in his world. If mankind had never had any experience of God, how did such a notion appear in its mind?

Engels in his day was ready with an answer to this question, saying that our concept of God is a fantastic reflection in our mind of social realities. Christians then tried hard to prove that Engels was wrong, that God is not a fantastic reflection, but that the notion about Him is an exact mirroring of divine reality. The time has come for another line of approach.

I admit that belief in God is a fantastic reflection, and I add that only the fantastic is real. All the "realism" that denied that men would ever be able to fly to the moon, or pilot a submarine under the ice of the North Pole, or annihilate distances by flying planes around the earth in a short time, or split the atom—all such "realism" has been proved wrong. Likewise, the "realism" of those who live in God's world and honestly assert that He does not exist is just as wrong. On the other hand, the fancies of Leonardo da Vinci and Jules Verne and others like them have become reality. And the dreamers of dreams who walk with a God you cannot see or touch, unless you develop the faculty of faith, perceive the reality which pervades all creation.

Only the fantastic is real in modern science. Niels Bohr asks, "Is anybody mad enough to have the truth?"

What is science? It is a discipline which makes the fantastic come true.

It has discovered that within the nucleus of a cell, in the DNA, is contained a code in which all former generations have transmitted to the new being their physical features. Now this knowledge had to pass outside the nucleus to where the proteins are built. So there is in the nucleus a kind of Xerox machine, which makes a photocopy of the DNA. And there is "somebody" who handles the Xerox machine.

A fantastic story! No novelist could have invented a better one. This fantasy is the truth about our organism.

Might religion also be a fantastic reflection? Then it is the right reflection of a fantastic reality and of its fantastic Creator.

Man's mind has a dualistic nature. It comprehends facts and it fancies. If it had not fancied, humanity would not have developed. Civilization is the fulfillment of what were formerly dreams. I would refuse a religion that consisted only of facts. It would not satisfy my dualistic nature. It must fulfill my desire after fancy, after myth.

Marx and Engels described facts, the terrible exploitation that existed under early capitalism. But they did not stop at this, because they were men. After the analysis of facts, fancy began to work: the dream of a new society without exploitation or wars, and with social justice. The fantasies of science have been fulfilled. A holy life, which is sheer fantasy for one who starts a life of faith, is achieved by many. But the Marxian society is still a Utopia. So Engels had no right to cast reproach on Christianity as belonging to fantasy—though we take this as a compliment.

You might reply that it is possible to imagine things that are beyond the realm of possibility. Thus you can fancy an island a mile square all made of diamonds in the midst of the ocean, yet such an island does not exist. But, everything you have "imagined" is real. In nature there are islands, there is the ocean, there are diamonds, and there exists the dimension of one mile square. Now, you have pieced together realities improperly, but it is only realities you could imagine. So in our mind the notion of God which we have can be associated with wrong ideas. I can believe in an evil God, a God in human form, a tribal or national God, and so on, but all the time I deal with realities, whether rightly or wrongly. God Himself exists and is what He is, not what we consider Him to be.

Engels did not have to tell us that our faith is absurd.

If God could fit within the frame of my reason, He would not be a God but a low being like myself. A philosopher whose philosophy could be understood by his five-year-old son would not be a philosopher. God, to be God, must transcend our reason by His deeds and by His being.

The atmosphere we breathe is a combination of nitrogen and oxygen perfectly suited to our lungs. The distance of the earth from the sun and the moon is just what is necessary for the maintenance of life, health, and happiness. The perpetual cycles of rain and snow make the earth fertile. The tides of the sea keep the shores clean and fresh. Vitamins necessary for bodily existence are provided in abundance. Laws and forces of nature stand ready to be harnessed for man's use. God has filled the earth with beauty and charm. There are majestic mountains and fertile valleys, tall trees and carpets of grass, the moonlight, the stillness of the desert, the thrill of songbirds—all of which witness to the fact that God made the earth for our pleasure.

If a young man loved a girl and presented her with a beautiful house surrounded by a splendid garden and told her, "This I have provided for you," the girl would have no doubt of the boy's love for her. This is just what has happened between God and us. He has made food to grow for us, and beneath the soil there are minerals and oil for tools and fuel. These are all evidences of God's provision for our needs and therefore of the actual existence of God.

Consider the bees, which organize a city with 10,000 cells for honey, 12,000 cells for larvae, filled with honey, and a place for the mother queen. When the bees observe that the heat is increasing and the wax may melt and the honey be lost, they organize the swarm into squads, put sentinels at the entrance, glue the feet down, and then with flying wings create a system of ventilation to cool the honey—something like an electric fan. Bees collect honey from an area of twenty square miles. Now, how can the tiny brain of a bee perform such wonders if behind it there is not a higher mind—the mind of God?

A group of scientists in Chicago did an experiment. A female moth of a rare species was placed in a room. Four miles away a male moth of the same species was released. In spite of the smoke of the city, in spite of the distance, and in spite of the fact that the female was in a closed room, within a few hours the male moth was found beating its wings against the window of the room in which the female was confined. Explain such a thing without an intelligent being—a God—who has created these things.

Fish lay their eggs in the fjords of Norway and from these eggs come a new generation of fish that somehow find their way across the ocean to the Caribbean Sea. When the time comes for them to spawn in their turn, they return to exactly the same fjords they had previously left. A man has to spend twenty years learning to become captain of a ship and to travel across the Atlantic Ocean. Who taught these fish to travel?

When we were in prison, the swallows made their nests in our cells, and every autumn they left our country. Yet these same swallows came back from as far as Mozambique to our prison in Romania, exactly to cell number twelve which they had left half a year before.

For those who have their eyes open, the wisdom and power of God are revealed in a million ways.

Does God exist? The question should not even be asked.

In every true rendering of the subject-predicate form, the predicate is contained in the subject. God is the ideal Being, the sum of all the highest qualities, such as love, goodness, righteousness, omnipotence, and so on. If He has all the perfections (which He must, or He would not be God), He must have existence, too. A nonexistent God would not have the sum of perfections. To ask, "Is there a God?" is tantamount to asking, "Is the existent existing?"

God is. With this conviction I live, and with this assertion I hope to die. I use the expression that God is, only because I am dealing with atheists. Otherwise it is senseless, a tautology, like "All bachelors are male." When you have said "bachelor," you have already said "male." And when you have said "God," His existence is implicit.

Prayer simply exists. How did mankind come by it? Where did this phenomenon originate? Nowhere. Men have always philosophized about God and have always sought communion with Him. Both philosophy and practical religion have been sometimes primitive, sometimes terribly false, but they were there.

An Indian tribe in North America prayed:

> O our mother earth, O our father heaven,
> we are your children.
> The sacrifices you ask for we offer
> with bent backs.

> Weave us a garment of radiant sunlight,
> the white dawn the warp,
> the red evening the woof.
> Let the murmuring rain be the fringe
> and the rainbow the hem.

> Weave us a garment of radiant sunlight,
> we want to walk where the birds sing.
> We want to walk through the green grass,
> O our mother earth, O our father heaven.

Augustine describes his experiences of praying as a young child:

> I was sent to school to learn how to read and
> write, things the usefulness of which I had no

idea. All the same, every time that I was slow to learn, I was beaten. God, my God, what misery I suffered there and how deceived I was!

We did, however, come into contact, Lord, with people who prayed to you. From them we learned—while we were, to the best of our ability, forming an impression of you—that you were someone great and powerful, able to hear us and to come to our help, even without revealing yourself to our senses. And it is true that, even as a small boy, I began to pray to you, my refuge and my help, and, calling on you, I lost all control of my tongue and, although I was a little person, I asked you with no little fervor that I might not be beaten any more at school.

Soviet soldiers, brought up in atheistic schools, prayed on the battlefront. Not knowing anything better, many of them prayed, "God and mother's spirit, help!" Old-time members of the Communist Party, who fell victim to the purges in Stalin's time, shared prison cells with us and told us that in difficult moments they prayed.

This prayer is a far cry from such lofty prayers as that of St. Gertrude: "Jesus, I am You; You are I. I am not You; You are not I. We both are together an entirely new being."

But men pray. I have known an atheistic lecturer who prayed to God for the success of his godless speeches, which were his means of earning a livelihood.

Dimly or consciously, men seek communion with God who exists, who is, who can be met. And if they persist, they meet Him.

25

PROPHECY

The authors of *The Atheist's Handbook* deny that any prophecy is possible. They dismiss prophecies "in the name of science." How is it then that Sir Isaac Newton, a scientist if ever there was one, the man who has been called "the father of reason," wrote a book called *Observations of Prophecies*? He is the one who provided the first really scientific chronology of a history of Jesus.

But instead of arguing whether prophecy is possible, let us analyze the facts. Facts if proven speak for themselves. Are there facts indicating that prophecies have been fulfilled?

Even a superficial knowledge of the Bible reveals hundreds of prophecies which have been fulfilled and others which are being fulfilled before our eyes.

First of all, there are the prophecies concerning Jesus Christ, who is the great subject of the Bible.

In the Bible, it was prophesied that Christ would be descended from Abraham and would belong to the tribe of Judah. The prophet Micah predicted seven centuries before the actual event that Christ would be born in the town of Bethlehem. Around the same time Isaiah told about his ministry of service and suffering and gave an outline of his life's story. The prophet Zechariah predicted that Jesus would enter Jerusalem humbly, riding on a donkey. Psalm 41 predicted His betrayal by one of His disciples. Zechariah told how much this traitor would get for his betrayal and what would happen with the money. The fact that Jesus would be whipped and spat upon was also predicted.

Some five centuries before Christ, the prophet Zechariah wrote that people would gaze on Him whom they had just pierced. David indicated that both His hands and His feet would be pierced. The resurrection of Jesus was predicted as well.

Granted that some of these prophecies can be ridiculed and written off by saying that their "fulfillment" was simply arranged by Jesus and His followers—such as His riding into Jerusalem on a donkey, or His cry on the cross, "I thirst" (John 19:28). But did the Roman soldiers deliberately set out to fulfill the prophecy contained in a psalm: "They divide my garments among them, and for my clothing they cast lots" (Psalm 22:18)? What did a Roman soldier know or care about Jewish prophecies? Yet each chronicler of the crucifixion meticulously recorded the detail about the soldiers casting lots for his garments, John adding the detail that the seamless robe was too valuable to be torn in pieces and divided among the four soldiers.

But how about the greatest event of all, Jesus' resurrection from the dead? Could He have staged that?

Even if He had been a great deceiver, as atheists like to allege, could He, under the watchful eyes of Jews and Romans alike, have arranged not to die on the cross, not to have His bones broken along with the thieves (in fulfillment of another explicit prophecy), not to succumb in the sealed, guarded tomb? And if He had managed thus far, could He have depended on His terrified, cowardly disciples to break through a band of soldiers, roll away the sealed stone, and release Him without hindrance? It is unthinkable.

Mommsen, the renowned historian of the Roman empire, calls the resurrection of the Savior the best established fact of Roman history. It could hardly have been staged by men. It was the fulfillment of prophecy.

26

PROPHECIES ABOUT THE JEWISH PEOPLE

"No prophecy," they say. Those whom we call prophets were just intelligent men and so were able to predict events.

According to *The Atheist's Handbook*, the most intelligent geniuses of mankind were Marx, Engels, Lenin, and others like them. They had in their minds what *The Atheist's Handbook* considers the most powerful means of understanding political and social events —that is, historic materialism.

Marx wrote a book called *The Jewish Question*. He obviously had the potential with which historic materialism endows a thinker. How is it that he, living in the second half of the nineteenth century, had no idea that the Jews, scattered as they were among the nations, would return to their land and have a country of their own? Lenin lived in the twentieth century. The Zionist movement was already in existence and was becoming stronger and stronger. He (the great genius of mankind) did not consider it likely at all that the Jews would be gathered together in their own land, nor did he, keen observer of everything in political life, armed with

168

the powerful weapon of historical materialism, even mention the Zionists. He neither took note of this movement nor expected it to triumph.

Stalin wrote a book entitled *The National Question*. In this book, which was written before the First World War, he who was once proclaimed by the atheists as the greatest genius mankind has ever had and will ever have, did not even acknowledge the Jews as a nation, because the Jewish people did not enter into his definition of what a nation is.

But the Jewish nation in its development disregarded both the anti-Semitism of the book of Marx and the fact that they were ignored in the book by Stalin. The Jews created a state, fulfilling what was predicted in quite another book—the one book which atheists despise above all others—the Bible.

Frederick the Great, King of Prussia, once asked his chaplain, "Give me a sure proof of the inspiration of the Holy Scriptures." The chaplain answered, "It is the Jew, Your Majesty." The Jews and their miraculous history are another proof of the truth of biblical prophecy.

Strangely enough, several of the authors of *The Atheist's Handbook* are Jews, fulfilling by this a biblical prophecy that some Jews would be a curse for all peoples. But there are also Jews who fight atheism and spread abroad the knowledge of God, thus fulfilling another prophecy in the same Bible which says that a remnant in Israel will in the last days turn to their Savior Jesus Christ and be a great blessing.

The prophecies about the Jews begin with a promise made to Abraham, the first Jew, some 4,500 years ago. Listen to it: "I will make of you a great nation" (Genesis 12:2).

The Christian world bears the name of a Jew, Jesus Christ. The Communist camp was founded upon the name of another Jew, Marx. The universe as a whole bears the name of yet another Jew, Einstein. Over sixty percent of the Nobel Prize winners are Jewish, among them the lamented Soviet writer, Boris Pasternak. Jews played a tremendous role in the Communist revolution—men like Trotsky, Zinoviev, Kamenev. Lenin was half-Jewish. Jews played a big role in the anti-government fight within the Soviet Union. Litvinov, the writer Daniel, Krasnov-Levitin, and other freedom fighters who have suffered imprisonment, are Jewish. Jews are active in the economic and political life of the United States and many other countries. They hold government positions in many Western nations. The Jew Teller is called "the father of the nuclear bomb."

Dr. Sale Harrison in his book *The Remarkable Jew* writes: "No one will doubt that the Jews of today hold the money chests of the world. Wherever they have gone, they have become the wizards of finance."

Basil Mowll says in his book *Bible Light in Present Events:* "A careful computation of the university professors of Western Europe, apart from Great Britain before the First World War, showed that about seventy percent were of Jewish birth and persuasion."

For the first time in history, a woman has been employed by the Roman Curia. She is a Christian of Jewish origin.

Simone Weil, a Jewess, was one of the most profound theologians of Catholicism.

The Hebrew language is the only old language that has been revived and is now spoken currently in Israel. This has not happened with Latin, old Greek, Slavonic, Irish, Welsh, or any other old language.

Thus, the prophecy has been fulfilled. A small Bedouin tribe has become a great nation—great in all aspects, for good or for ill. Even Yaroslavski, founder and president of the League of the Godless and the great leader of this movement, was Jewish.

The prophecy continues, "You will be a blessing" (Genesis 12:2). Whoever feels blessed by communism owes it to the Jew Marx. Whoever feels blessed by capitalism owes it to the Jews who were instrumental in creating this system. Whoever is blessed by Christianity owes it to a Jew, Jesus.

The Word of God says also in the same chapter, "I will bless those who bless you, and him who dishonors you I will curse" (Genesis 12:3). It is a simple fact that history has favored the friends of the Jews. When Spain expelled the Jews, the sun set on its empire. Czarist Russia persecuted Jews and has had its reward. So did Nazi Germany. Countries where the Jews are free enjoy freedom themselves.

Long after Abraham's day there were predictions that the Jews would be scattered among the nations. Today there are three scattered races—the Gypsies, the Armenians, and the Jews—but it is the Jews who are the most widely scattered. There are few countries without Jews.

Jesus predicted the destruction of Jerusalem, which took place in the year AD 70. The prophet Hosea predicted: "My God will reject them because they have not listened to him; they shall be wanderers among the nations" (Hosea 9:17); and so they have become. In Deuteronomy 28:37 it was written: "You shall become a horror, a proverb, and a byword among all the peoples where the LORD will lead you away"; and so they have become. It is a common form of mockery to say "Dirty Jews."

But the return of the Jews to Palestine was also predicted, and this has happened before our eyes. The tribe of the Book, of the wandering foot and the weary breast, again has its fatherland.

The Bible says repeatedly that the Jews are intended by God to remain a unique people—and this they really are.

The origins of other peoples are wrapped in legends and myth. Can anyone tell who was the first Russian? Or who was the first German or Turk? Ask any Jew who was the first Jew, and he will unhesitatingly reply, "Abraham."

The Jews are unique as a witness to the reliability of the biblical records. Unique is their dispersion among all the nations; equally unique is their development. The Jews are only one-half percent of the population of the world, yet how disproportionate is their suffering. They are unique also in their deliverance, their return to their own country, and the fact that their whole history has been foretold. God said through Moses: "I will scatter you among the nations, and I will unsheathe the sword after you, and your land shall be a desolation, and your cities shall be a waste" (Leviticus 26:33). "And the LORD will scatter you among the peoples, and you will be left few in number among the nations where the LORD will drive you" (Deuteronomy 4:27).

Later, another prophecy foretells the gathering of the scattered people of Israel: "I will take you from the nations and gather you from all the countries and bring you into your own land" (Ezekiel 36:24).

The Jews are unique in that they have remained apart, while scattered throughout the whole world. Wherever the Jew is found, he is a Jew. He is not a Jewish Russian, but a Russian Jew. The Jews remain Jews, although they have no concentrating force and no worldwide government.

They are the only people who could not be destroyed through unique sufferings. Egyptian pharaohs, Assyrian kings, Roman emperors, the Crusaders, the Inquisitors, and the Nazis have used against them expatriation, exile, captivity, confiscation, torture, the massacre of millions—all of which would have broken the heart of any other people—but the Jews remain.

God promised that He would assemble the outcasts of Israel and gather the dispersed of Judah from the four corners of the earth. This was said by Isaiah, who lived some 700 years before Christ and some 800 years before the dispersion of the Jews after the destruction of Jerusalem. How could he have known that the Jews would be dispersed and then gathered from all the continents?

Very few of the Jews who have returned to Israel are religious. Most of them do not know the Scriptures and the prophecies, and of those who know them, a very limited number have faith in them. Yet they are brought back—you may call it by blind impulse, just as the birds are drawn to the south for the winter—or, to put it in other words, the power of God is driving them in order that His word may be fulfilled.

In another important prophecy in which the return of the Jews to Palestine is mentioned, it is said that they will come by two methods (Jeremiah 16:14–16).

God will send "fishermen" who will "fish" them, and the Zionist movement "fished" many thousands of Jews with the bait of a national home of their own.

The same verse also says that God will send many "hunters" who will "hunt" the Jews. The anti-Semitism in the whole world, especially under Hitler, has "hunted" the Jews, driving them toward Palestine.

Another startling prophecy about the Jews concerns their turning to Christ in the end-time of the remnant of the people of Israel. This also is in the process of being fulfilled.

I have already quoted the Jew Einstein as an admirer of the Nazarene.

Franz Werfel, the famous Jewish poet, wrote a renowned Christian book, *The Song of Bernadette*. Sholom Asch, the great Jewish novelist, became a Christian and wrote the well-known book *Jesus of Nazareth*. Martin Buber, the great Jewish philosopher, called Jesus "my great brother." Henri Bergson has proclaimed his Christian faith. Niels Bohr, the great physicist, was a Hebrew Christian. So was Auguste Piccard, the man who first went into the stratosphere.

27

PROPHECIES ABOUT
THE LATTER DAYS

The Atheist's Handbook dismisses prophecy with these words: "Numerous biblical prophecies have been made only after the predicted events have happened. The respective texts have been included in the Bible *post factum*—that is, after the consummation of the respective events."

Now, do our atheist friends really expect us to believe that the victory of Israel in history, the waving of the Zionist flag on Hitler's Brown House in Nurenberg, and the restoration of the Jewish state—all events of the twentieth century—have only recently been included in the Bible? Do not the Dead Sea Scrolls, dating from the century before Christ, testify to the great age of the prophecies? Do not New Testament manuscripts contain the prediction of the fisherman Peter that the elements will melt with great heat, thus foreshadowing nuclear destruction?

World wars were not possible 3,000 years ago, since communication among continents was nonexistent, except perhaps on a very primitive scale.

But the prophet Jeremiah, who lived some six hundred years before Christ, predicted world wars. He did not know that America or Australia or Japan existed, but he wrote about "a sword against all the inhabitants of the earth . . . disaster is going forth from nation to nation . . . those pierced by the Lord on that day shall extend from one end of the earth to the other" (Jeremiah 25:29–33).

The prediction was fulfilled after twenty-six centuries. Thousands upon thousands of people were slain in a war which extended from Japan to Russia to France, a war in which such people as Americans and Chinese and Germans and Jews all died. And these things are the forebodings of the next world conflagration.

Jesus said about the last days: "Then there will be great tribulation, such as has not been from the beginning of the world until now, no, and never will be" (Matthew 24:21). And so it is. Never in the history of mankind have there been such tribulations as those created by the ovens and gas chambers of the Nazis and the mass-slaughter of Stalin or Mao Tse-Tung.

When Christ said, "If those days had not been cut short, no human being would be saved" (Matthew 24:22), there did not exist any means of destruction which could endanger all flesh. Men had arrows and spears. Nobody could endanger the existence of all mankind. Now the instruments of general destruction are available.

But why go so far? In a general sense, communism itself is a fulfillment of prophecy. It is like the great Antichrist predicted in the Scriptures: "It was allowed to make war on the saints and to conquer them. And authority was given it over every tribe and people and language and nation" (Revelation 13:7).

Another prophet has described powers like that of communism. He says that their greed is as wide as Sheol and, like death, they never have enough; they gather all nations and collect all peoples for themselves (Habakkuk 2:5).

We Christians find this ambition unreasonable. Was Stalin a happy man when he imposed his will on one billion men and was cheered as the greatest genius? His wife committed suicide. He jailed members of his own family. He had no confidence in anyone, not even in his nearest comrades, and this with good cause. His closest henchmen waited for his death to denounce him as a criminal. Khrushchev says that Stalin once exclaimed, "I don't have confidence even in myself!"

Happiness does not consist in dominating the world, but in knowing God. Our Communist friends do not know this secret. Therefore they have vast ambitions, but are never satisfied and are ever further from the Utopia they claim to be creating.

In the end Jesus will return. His feet will stand on the Mount of Olives in Israel. The Bible tells us, "Every eye will see him" (Revelation 1:7). This again must have appeared incomprehensible when John the Evangelist wrote it. How could somebody in Spain or in Northern Africa have seen Jesus ascending from the Mount of Olives and how will they be able to see Him descend again in like manner?

Well, television proves the prophecy of the Bible to be true. The whole world witnessed the Olympic games as they took place. The whole world will witness the return of Jesus.

And then, at the name of Jesus, every knee shall bow, of things in heaven and things on earth and things under the earth, and every tongue shall confess that Jesus Christ is Lord, to the glory of God the Father.

The blessed day will come when all authority will reside in the hands of Jesus Christ, after His return to the earth, and under His total rule our poor planet will be rid of its sins and of its sorrows.

Before that time, we first have to past through terrible catastrophes. Among the signs of approaching calamity are the many peace conferences and talks about arms limitations, which are also predicted in the Bible: "While people are saying, 'There is peace and security,' then sudden destruction will come upon them as labor pains come upon a pregnant woman, and they will not escape" (1 Thessalonians 5:3).

When the apostle Paul wrote this prophecy, men had no means to bring sudden destruction upon the earth. It could not be accomplished with swords or spears. Now nations possess nuclear weapons.

Prophecy becomes exceptionally important in these days. Jesus had predicted that the Gentiles will dominate Jerusalem "until the times of the Gentiles are fulfilled" (Luke 21:24). The fact that in 1967 the Jews got sovereignty over all of Jerusalem and Palestine might be a first sign that the time of the Gentiles—that is, the time when the Gentiles (the non-Jews) can join the Church of Christ and thus be saved for eternity—is near its end. It is most urgent that people should believe in Christ and should come to Him while there is time. It is a satanic device that just in this epoch, atheists should spread doubt about the validity and existence of prophecy.

Their attempt is itself a tragic fulfillment of a biblical prophecy: "The word of the cross is folly to those who are perishing" (1 Corinthians 1:18).

Christians never doubt the prophecies because they find that many apply to themselves and their lives. When we become Christians, we find that this was prophesied long ago. We read in the Bible that God chose us before the foundation of the world to belong to Christ Jesus. How far into the past this prophecy reaches!

Then we find our future prophesied: "That in the coming ages [God] might show the immeasurable riches of his grace in kindness toward us in Christ Jesus" (Ephesians 2:7). So we know what the meaning of our life is and that God's goodness is in store for us.

28

WHO MADE GOD?

There is a God. We can have communion with Him. He has revealed Himself through His prophets and His Son, Jesus Christ.

Nature is like a banquet. There are bananas and melons and tomatoes and wheat. But there can be no banquet without a cook. Nor can there be a world without a Creator. This is the best argument for the existence of God.

But our opponents have the right to answer with another question. If everything must have a cause and you call the cause God, God must also have a cause. Who created Him? It would be a subterfuge to evade the answer by saying that the question is blasphemous. I find it most legitimate. I myself asked it as a child.

All mass or matter is continually in movement. It is not now exactly the same as it was one second ago. There is always a cause which has produced a change. The movement of matter is measured by time. In time, some states of matter produce effects which, in their turn, become causes of new changes. Matter is inconceivable without a first cause.

But existence in time is not the only form of existence. There exists also timelessness, in which there is no before and no after;

no cause and no effect. This is the realm of God. He has created everything. He belongs to a sphere of self-existence. Nobody created Him.

Which came first, the chicken or the egg? This is the classic question. If the egg, who laid it? If the hen, from where did it come? You can discuss the dilemma for thousands of years without coming to any conclusion if you do not realize that the original question has three presuppositions:

1) There is a hen.

2) There is an egg.

3) There is a "first" and an "after."

"First" and "after" are categories of our thinking, forms for our sensitivity, manners in which we apprehend the successive stages of matter in continual movement. But time is nothing apart from the movements it serves to measure. Time has no objective existence, independent of bodies and phenomena; this is the ABC of Einstein's theory of relativity. Kinetic energy produces movement and gives birth to the notion of time. What about the huge realm of potential energy? It lies dormant. Imagine a world with only potential energy. There would not be the slightest movement, there would be nothing to measure. It would be a universe without time. Timeless is also the sphere of Spirit, the realm of God. We call Him eternal. Eternity is not endless time, but timelessness.

Let us try to exemplify the meaning of the above.

Suppose that on a planet some 2,000 light-years away, there were beings of a much higher order than ourselves with telescopes that could enable them to see not only our earth, but also its inhabitants.

Suppose these super-beings should look today at Bethlehem. What would they see? The birth of Jesus Christ. They would see the shepherds, the Magi, Mary, Joseph, the Babe—this because it would take the light from these persons two thousand years to arrive at the distant planet. For us, the birth of Christ is a past event. For them, it would happen today.

Imagine such super-beings on a star 3,500 light-years away! They would see the children of Israel, under the leadership of Moses, approaching the borders of Palestine. They would see them rejoicing at the announcement that a Savior would be born. For them, the birth of Jesus would be a future event.

One and the same event is past from the point of view of earth, present for one planet, and future for another. How is it for the spirit which can apprehend simultaneously what is happening on all three planets and read the minds of all? There is no past, present, and future.

The question "Which came first, the chicken or the egg?" is solved. There is no first and no later. The problem has no sense in a realm where there is no past or future, cause or effect. The problem "Who was before God to create Him?" cannot be posed. There is no before.

Our "now" has no value for cosmic phenomena, as it has no value for what happens within the atom. What we capture at this moment as stellar images in observatories are rays of light from stars which might have disappeared ages ago.

Einstein writes, "Each frame of time or system of coordinates has its own time." And, "Unless the body to which a statement of time refers is specified, there is no significance in the statement of the time of an event." For the eternal Spirit, there is no time. Here everything is interrelated and forms a unity. God is one. The whole of reality created by Him is one single gravitational field. When we arrive at the point Omega, the continual agitation measured by time is changed into blessed contemplation, into the ecstasy and rapture of adoration.

There is a story about a monk who was sent by his abbot on an errand in the forest. There for a few seconds he heard a bird from Paradise. When he returned to the monastery, the doorkeeper did not recognize him. The abbot and the other monks were all foreigners to him. Nobody knew him. Finally, someone remembered that the monastery possessed an ancient record telling about a monk who had gone into the woods many centuries before and had never returned. For him only a few seconds had passed; he had caught something of the beauty of the music of Paradise. For the others, in the meantime, centuries had elapsed.

This medieval legend has become today strict scientific fact in the so-called paradox of Langevin.

It is obvious that the time which elapses during the passage of a train between two stakes is less for an observer who travels in the train than for an observer at rest alongside the track. For the former, time is shorter. The time is shorter not only for him, but for everything which is in the train, including his watch, which slows down.

Imagine now a rocket traveling near the speed of light. Earth dwellers recording the beating of the astronaut's heart would find that it had slowed down. The same would happen with the movements within the body of the astronaut, though for the astronaut himself, they would have remained the same.

According to Langevin's unchallengeable calculation, a man leaving the earth at a speed inferior to that of light by a twenty thousandth, traveling for a year of his own time and returning at the same speed to land on the globe (i.e., two years after his departure measured by his own clock), would return two centuries later according to our calendar. The great-grandson of his daughter, born on the day of departure when the astronaut was thirty years old, would be one hundred years old, whereas he himself would be thirty-two.

Such a rocket is not pure fancy. There exists one for which even the speed of light is child's play. It is the rocket of the spirit. In mere seconds, my thought passes from galaxies far away to my old mother, from there to Paradise, from Paradise to a cell nearby on the same prison-corridor, from there back to remote stars. Then I pass to communion with Adam and Abel, but I can leave them at once and pass my time in future millenniums, to return to my cell and eat the dinner which has just been served. The spirit is not bound by space or time. Death happens in time. In time events succeed one another. I have been born, I have developed, I will die, I will be resurrected. In the sphere of timelessness, things do not happen successively. There is no place left for a passing away of my personality.

If I travel in a train with uniform speed in a given direction, I have the impression that towns and villages pass near me. I can see them through the window as an endless stream of localities. But as a matter of fact, the localities coexist simultaneously. Only to me do they appear in succession. In the cinema, I see the lives of several persons developing from birth to death, with all their complications. But in the cabin of the operator, on a reel, these events coexist all together. Only for me do they happen successively in time.

We are used to the limitations of weight. It was quite a discovery when the first astronauts realized that they could also live in a state of weightlessness. We live in time, in which things appear and disappear. Therefore we believe in death and dissolution. But there exists the sphere of timelessness as well, the sphere of God. He is the uncreated Author of all creation. In Him, we have from eternity to eternity our life, existence, and movement. While we are in time, we live reality as if it were composed of successive events. But to apply our notion of time to the spirit is as foolish as to apply it to nuclear physics.

According to the theory of relativity, at the speed of light every clock stops, with mass presenting an infinite inertia to every effort to accelerate it. Is it not therefore reasonable that in the Bible God is called "light" and Christians are called "the light of the world" (John 8:12; Matthew 5:14)?

Now, everyone simply bows when he hears the name of Einstein, but my opponents would do well to remember that Lenin assailed the principle of relativity, that Mach who inspired the works of Einstein had been denounced by Lenin as the Judas of science, and that for a long time Soviet philosophers discarded Einstein and the whole realm of cybernetics.

29

LIFE AFTER DEATH

Atheists don't know what life is. The Russian academician Oparin says, "Life is one of the forms of movement of matter." What should a young man do with such a definition? He asks his atheist father, "How should I believe in life? How can I best use my life?" But his father cannot possibly give him an answer, because he has really asked how one of the forms of movement of matter with its intrinsic, unalterable laws should behave. How much more powerful is the Christian's answer: "Life is a person, Jesus Christ, whose friendship you can accept and whose example you can follow. Life is an eternal boon. Its earthly span is to be used unsparingly for others, and its eternal aftermath in Paradise—to which earth is the anteroom—for one's enjoyment of his Creator and His glory."

Not knowing what life is, atheists don't know what death is. Therefore death is a terror, devoid of the comforts and hopes of religion. It is cold comfort to say to the bereaved, "Well, one dies and disappears for ever." But humanity is moving ahead.

In his own bereavement, Marx wrote in a letter to Lassalee, "The death of my son has shaken me deeply, and I feel the loss as keenly as though it were only yesterday, and my poor wife has completely broken down under the blow."

We sympathize with his feelings. He did not know the Christian's triumph over death.

For atheists death is like the sword of Damocles hanging over their heads, reminding them that soon all their joys—or sorrows!—will be gone.

Death holds no fear for those who know.

Jesus asserted, "Everyone who lives and believes in me shall never die" (John 11:26). He said it near the grave of one who had believed in Him. Jesus proved right. Birth and death are our manner of apprehending the reality of life from the perspective of time. Christians do not have to fear death.

During the Russian Revolution in the great terror under the Tcheka, a group of Christians were ordered to be drowned. One of them exclaimed, "We go to God! What difference if we go by land or sea?" They did not fear.

The Atheist's Handbook denounces belief in life beyond the grave as "the basis of the religious theory" and "extremely dangerous."

But what is life if nothing follows after death?

Let us suppose that Socialist ideals are accomplished. We will have a perfect society, without the distinction between rich and poor, without wars and revolutions, with wealth, culture, and happiness for everybody. But men will still have to die. Poor men die easily. There is not much to lose. For happy men death is a catastrophe. Kirov, general secretary of the Communist Party of the Leningrad district, assassinated by Stalin, had a position of power. He enjoyed life. His last words were, "I wish to live and to live and to live." If Stalin had not killed him, he would have died a natural death a few years later and his last tragic words would have been the same.

We all have to die. The decision does not depend on us. If nothing follows, the most beautiful life is nothing more than a banquet offered to a condemned man before his execution. He gets dainties and then he is hanged. He may live in an ideal society, but eventually he will rot, forgotten forever by everyone.

Go, comfort somebody who is dying in a cancer ward, or his family, with these words: "We are building a happy Socialist society," or "Science achieves great things. We have been to the moon and soon we will be on Venus." There is not much consolation in this. But tell the dying and the bereaved about the heavenly Father and the Christian's hope of living eternally with Him, and you will see the difference.

If the atheists are right and there is no life hereafter, "All our yesterdays have lighted fools the way to dusty death," and, "Life is but a poor player that struts and frets his hour upon the stage and then is heard no more. It is a tale told by an idiot, full of sound and fury, signifying nothing" (Shakespeare).

But life continues after death. The thought of eternity and reward for good and evil is deeply inscribed in the human heart.

Christians sacrifice themselves because they believe in eternal life. But some atheists sacrifice themselves, too, for some national or social ideal. Why do they die for a noble cause? Christians believe in an eternal recompense. But what sense does it make for an atheist to give up this life, the only one he knows he has, for an ideal whose fulfillment he cannot check on, and whose beauties he will not enjoy? They would never sacrifice their lives if, in the depths of their soul to which reason has no access, they did not know that the grave is not the end and that those who have spent their all for some great good will be rewarded.

All modern science is based on the law of conservation of energy, as expounded by Lavoisier. Nothing is lost, nothing is added, everything is conserved. (This law ceases to apply strictly only within the atom.)

Man is a bundle of energy in different forms: energy condensed in matter, heat, electricity, and spiritual energy. What happens to these different forms of energy at death? The energy condensed in atoms is not lost. The body decays and its atoms enter into new combinations. The heat of the body is not lost. When the oven waxes cold, its heat has been communicated to the surrounding atmosphere. By a minimal, immeasurable fraction of a degree, the temperature of the atmosphere around us increases when our bodies become cold corpses. The electricity emanating from the body reenters into the general budget of electrical energy in nature. What happens to spiritual energy at death, to the power to will, the capacity to think and to feel? Does this energy change at death, transformed into a lower form of energy, say, the mechanical? If so, we would be able after death to jump twice as high as we did before, which is ridiculous. No! Spiritual energy remains after death. Otherwise, the law of Lavoisier collapses.

If our spirit is prepared for this event, if it has invested in the things of value in the eternal realm—love, truth, faith, hope, peace, gentleness, meekness (Galatians 5:22,23; Philippians 4:8,9; 1 Corinthians 3:12–15)—it will be in its own element. The future life will be a paradise of enjoyment of things hoped for. If our spirit enters that realm completely unprepared, full of sins and a craving for lustful satisfactions which cannot be fulfilled, our unfulfilled cravings will increase our suffering in hell.

As imperceptibly as vapor mounts in the air, the life expires. But the vapor does not cease to exist; neither does the spirit. The apostle James writes, "What is your life? For you are a mist that appears for a little time and then vanishes" (James 4:14). But it does not go off into nothing. Steam turns into water. Nothing is ever lost. Earthly life passes away, but it does not become nothing. A caterpillar becomes a cocoon, a cocoon a butterfly. Dead men have passed out of our sight. It does not mean that they do not exist anymore.

Suppose we could speak with an embryo and tell it that the life it leads in its mother's womb is only a preparatory one. The real life follows in another world unknown to the embryo, in conditions unimaginable to him. The embryo would answer like *The Atheist's Handbook*, if it had the intelligence of an academician: "Don't bother me with these religious superstitions! The life in the womb is the only one I know, and there is no other. Sheer inventions of greedy clergymen!"

But suppose this embryo could think with greater discernment than our academicians. It would say to itself, "Eyes develop in my head. To what purpose? There is nothing to see. Legs grow. I do not even have room to stretch them. Why should they grow? And why do arms and hands grow? I have to keep them folded over my breast. They embarrass me and my mother. My whole development in the womb is senseless unless there follows a life with light and color and many objects for my eyes to see. The place in which I'll spend this other life must be large and varied. I will have to run in it. Therefore my legs grow. It will be a life of work and struggle. Therefore I grow arms and fists, which are of no use here." Reflections on his own development would lead an embryo to the knowledge of another life, though he had no experience of it.

This is exactly our situation, too. The church of Christ teaches us that life in this world also has an embryonic character and is only a preparation for the real life which follows. How do we know that? If God (or nature, for the sake of argument) had created us only for this life, we would have been given first the wisdom and experience of old age and then the vigor of youth. We would have known how to live. But the fact is that while we are vigorous young men and women, we lack wisdom and more often than not throw away our years on nothing. When we have accumulated wisdom and experience, the funeral hearse is waiting outside our door. Then why do we accumulate wisdom? Well, why do eyes and legs and hands grow on the embryo? Only for what follows. Our development in this life points to a future one.

Body and spirit have not only separate but contradictory developments. As we grow in age, our body decays and our spirit is enriched. Spirit and body are like two travelers, one ascending a mountain, the other descending it. They travel in opposite directions. Which logic will make me believe that when the body has arrived at the bottom of the mountain, at the final decay, the spirit will decay with it? Is it not much more likely that, after a steep ascension, it will soar to the heaven of heavens.

I passed many years in solitary confinement, without books. I passed my time imagining all kinds of situations: that I was the president of the Soviet Republics, the king of England, the pope, a millionaire, a beggar. I could imagine all such situations. They are imaginable because they are possibilities of life. Life is rich. It could make out of a corporal a French emperor and of this emperor a prisoner on an island. Poor men have become millionaires. Rich men have become paupers. Stalin, son of a heavy-drinking shoe-maker, a Georgian and former seminarian, became dictator not only of the Soviet Union, but also of the whole Communist bloc. Shortly after his death, his name was erased from history. All such things are possible in life and therefore can also be imagined. But I tried to imagine that I was dead, and I never succeeded because death is not one of the possibilities of life.

If you try very hard to fancy yourself dead, the last thing you imagine is that you see yourself stretched out immobile in a coffin in a funeral chapel. The fact that you see yourself in the coffin shows that you are not dead. A dead man does not see himself. The unimaginability of death is no slight argument in favor of the eternity of human life.

The important thing is not to confound eternity with endless time, which is a contradiction in terms. Endless time does not exist! Eternity is timelessness.

We can have a glimpse of this in the possibilities of dream life, in which mental operations are sometimes performed with extreme rapidity. A series of acts which normally would occupy a great length of time pass through our minds in an instant during a dream. The relationships of space are also abolished. We can traverse huge distances in a second. We are not bound by space and time in a dream and, pondering on the dream life, we realize that the walls of space and time which imprison us while we are awake, hide from us another quality of life beyond the limited sphere which we call "reality."

The human body to be fully satisfied needs very few things: food, clothing, shelter, rest, and at a certain age, a partner of the other sex. How is it then that atheists who have plenty of all of these are sometimes melancholy and dissatisfied? How is it that people imprisoned for their beliefs—hungry, shivering with the cold, in chains, separated for years from their beloved ones—can exult for joy? What is the mysterious entity which can be depressed while the body has all good things and can rejoice while the body passes through sufferings? It is something other than the body. This is the soul.

It shows its interdependence on, but also its independence from, the body during our earthly life. It is so independent from the body that it can decide on suicide. The soul can decide to kill its own body for psychological reasons. There is no reason to believe that the death of the body must also imply the death of this strong-willed, independent entity.

In the Second Book of Kings in the Bible, there is a curious expression. There are enumerated different objects which King

Solomon had constructed for the temple. The enumeration ends with the words, "The brass of all these vessels was without weight" (25:16, KJV).

Is there brass without weight? Even a feather has weight. Only when we think about specific objects, we consider weight. That is, a specific piece of brass, a certain feather, each has weight. Brass as a generalization has no weight.

Scholastic philosophy was correct in distinguishing between the essence of an object and its forms. The essence of bread is that it is an object made of dough which serves for food. This essence has no weight. Bread can have different shapes and ingredients. It can be barley bread, wheat bread, fresh or old bread, a small or a big loaf of bread. The weight, color, and size will vary accordingly. Bread is a notion in my spirit. There it is weightless, until it has taken a specific form. So is brass, if it does not have a certain size and shape.

Even then, objects have weight only under the pull of gravity. In a spacecraft, in a state of weightlessness, objects float around. Unaffected by gravity, they have no weight.

King Solomon had constructed a spiritual temple. No Babylonian soldier could carry away what he had constructed in his mind to the honor of the Lord.

In the Soviet Union, on September 1, 1968, a law was enacted according to which children can be taken away from parents and placed in atheistic boarding schools if they are taught the Christian faith. Christian parents endure this pressure. From the Sloboda family three children were taken away; from the Malozemlov family seven. Who can separate a man with spiritual thinking from his child?

There is the essence "child" and there are the images. The latter vary. My child has been an embryo; then a baby; then a child who played with toys. I can hold the child in my arms, or it can be far away. It can be an obedient child or a child who has gone astray. The images can change. The fact that it is my child never changes. The relationship of parent/child belongs to the realm of essence. We are not afraid of what the Communists do to the children. The parent/child relationship never changes.

The same applies to life. Which life can perish at death?

I have had a rich life and a poor one, a joyous life and a sad one, the life of a free man and that of a prisoner, the life of a healthy man and that of a sick man. If I identify myself with one of the forms of life, my life ceases when that particular form of life ceases. For some men, life loses its value when they have no more luxury.

But we Christians live in the essential.

Jesus says, "I am the way, and the truth, and the life" (John 14:6). The word "am" is not used in Hebrew, the language which Jesus spoke, just as it is not used in Russian. He said, "I—the way, the truth, and the life." He identifies Himself with abstract notions.

Nature knows only oaks and pines and apple trees. "Tree" is an abstraction formed in my mind. You can destroy all the trees of the world. The notion "tree" will not be touched by this catastrophe.

In nature, there are only real men, Grigoriev and Ivanov and Gherasimov, a Russian, a Ukrainian, an American, a poor man, a rich man, a female, a male. There are real lives spent selfishly or sacrificially. There can be active or contemplative lives.

Jesus does not identify Himself with one certain kind of life, but with the abstract notion "life," with life containing all possibilities. He teaches us to do the same. I do not identify my life with Wurmbrand, born some sixty-five years ago and subject to death. I have life which has always existed in God, which has taken the form of human life with Adam and Eve, the life which will never end. My life, as a child of God, is indestructible.

The body is not my "I." In a sense, I have had many bodies— that of an embryo, that of a babe, that of a child, that of a young man. The apostle Peter writes, "I am in this tent" (KJV). He refers to his body at a certain stage. I have lived in several tents, but there is a clear-cut distinction between me and the habitation in which I live for a time.

Jesus says in the Garden of Gethsemane, "My soul is very sorrowful" (Mark 14:34). Pay attention to his expression! Everyone else could use it. He speaks about a soul and about a possessor of the soul who observes the soul and establishes that it is sorrowful. But I am not identical with a certain state of my soul either, as I am not identical with a certain state of my body.

I suffer in my body or in my soul. I know that I suffer. I know enough to know that I suffer. What is the last reality in me that observes everything that happens to what I consider "the real me"? He knows "I am healthy now," or "I die now." Who is the one who knows and observes all these changes? He Himself is unchanged.

He is not a life, but the Life—the Son of God within, the One who cannot die.

Jesus said, "I am the truth." How can a truth ever disappear? If I identify myself like Him with truth, with all truth, the whole truth, who will be able to destroy me? It is axiomatic that 2 + 2 = 4 whether I am in prison or at liberty, alive or dead. I become one with the truth, which is independent of external events.

If I unite with Christ, if I take for myself the words, "I am the way, the truth, and the life," I will live eternally.

The lowest organisms in the ladder of life are unicellular. They multiply by division. One becomes two, two become four, and so on. There are now myriads of amoebas. But did the first amoeba ever die? It has changed its form of existence. Instead of being within one membrane, it has multiplied infinitely. Every day, millions of amoebas die, but they all are only parts of the first amoeba. The first amoeba thus lives on in them. Deathlessness appears already on the first step of the ladder of organism. And should the highest being we know on earth simply pass away?

We treasure with great care a painting by Leonardo da Vinci and a sculpture by Michelangelo. And should the Creator not keep with at least the same care the artists who produced these works?

There is an eternal life, and as an unrepentant Hitler cannot very well spend it in the same place as the innocent children he killed, there must be a heaven for the just and a hell for the unjust.

Atheists do wrong to live as if they will never die. How do they know that at the last minute they will not regret having led astray millions of men by their godless teachings?

Let them learn from the dying words of great adversaries of the Christian religion. Talleyrand: "I am suffering the pangs of the damned." Mirabeau: "Give me laudanum that I may not think of eternity." Voltaire: "I am abandoned by God and man. I shall go to hell. Oh, Christ, oh, Jesus Christ!" Charles IX, King of France: "What blood, what murders, what evil counsels have I followed. I am lost, I see it well." Thomas Paine: "I would give worlds, if I had them, if *The Age of Reason* [an anti-Christian book] had never been published. Oh, Lord, help me. Christ, help me. Stay with me. It is hell to be left alone."

I hope to have proved at least that belief in eternal life is not as ridiculous as atheists wish to indicate.

There was an international symposium of doctors that discussed which operation is the most difficult. A German said that it was brain surgery, a Frenchman heart surgery. Our Soviet delegate said that the most difficult operation was a tonsillectomy. All laughed, but he said, "You consider my assertion stupid. You forget that since the Revolution, we have to extract tonsils through the brain, after trepanation of the skull, because we are forbidden to open the mouth."

We may open our mouths without the permission of governments. Once Christians speak out, it is seen that they are right.

30

SCIENCE AND RELIGION

The Communist Secret Police in the USSR were renowned for their ability to squeeze out confessions of imaginary crimes from innocent persons. Thousands of such "criminals" were rehabilitated under Khrushchev. But the methods have not changed.

Among the prisoners tortured by the atheists is a certain comrade "Science." Beaten, burned with red-hot iron pokers, or mistreated in some other manner, this prisoner with the name of "Science" has made sensational confessions, reproduced in *The Atheist's Handbook*. No real scientist would give a dime for them. Just listen to a few:

"Science has demonstrated in an unchallengeable manner that supernatural forces do not exist. [We poor, ignorant clods believed that science can demonstrate only existing things.] Science demonstrates that life is largely spread in the universe... The number of planets on which beings endowed with reason live is infinitely large... The scientific thesis about the multitude of inhabited worlds gives a mortal blow to the dogma of atonement, which is the essence of Christianity... The nonexistence of miracles has been fully demonstrated," and so on.

We have to discard this whole section as rubbish. Let us pass to other assertions.

It is an axiom for atheists that between science and religion there is an irreconcilable conflict. Between which science and which religion? Both are entities in continuous development.

What God has revealed is eternal. What men have thought about this revelation is transitory.

But science also changes.

Our opponents resort to an old trick: they compare modern science with primitive religion, science of the twentieth century after Christ with religious notions of the Jews of 3,500 years ago, when they had just escaped from centuries of slavery, were illiterate, and lived on a much lower cultural level than the gypsies of today. But this is dishonest.

Science of today has to be compared with the highest religious thought of today, and then we will see coincidence rather than conflict.

And that is as it should be. We will again quote Einstein: "Most people say that it is the intellect which makes a great scientist. They are wrong; it is the character." Now, character is not a scientific but a religious and moral value. Nobody can be a real scientist without having a character based on honesty and integrity. These are the values which Christianity teaches.

A man who has only science is not reliable as a scientist. He must have sincerity; he must believe in what he discovers in his laboratory. He must have hope, because without this he would never devote his time to research. He must have enthusiasm, otherwise he would not spend countless hours in the laboratory. He must have the humility simply to accept the order of things. There must be singleness of purpose, because if he were to scatter his interests, he would discover nothing. A scientist must be able to cooperate with his fellow scientists in the same laboratory. Patience is needed, like that of Madame Curie, who purified eight tons of pitchblende to extract a few milligrams of radium. There must be judgment, right judgment. He must tell the world exactly what he has found without a bit of exaggeration. He must also be wise and self-sacrificing, hiding what is detrimental for mankind. A man who is only a scientist is not a scientist. He must first of all accept the ethical values which not atheism but religion has given to mankind.

Stalin proclaimed, "Science is the savior of humanity." This he said just at the dawn of the atomic age, when science provided the tools for destroying in a moment whole cities, and the weapons by which humanity can be entirely blotted out. This, all because some of the scientists did not respect the values on which the whole edifice of science is built. Science must remain closely connected to religion, otherwise it will be impotent to help us achieve happiness. Because there has not always been this intimate collaboration between science and religion, humanity lives with less confidence in peace today than before the great discoveries of this modern age.

Even atheism is not possible without the ethical values of Christianity, as curious as this assertion may sound.

Authors of *The Atheist's Handbook* write: "The materialist conception says that in the world there exists nothing except eternal and infinite matter in movement." If there exists nothing but matter, then the materialistic philosophy, which says that everything is matter, must also be matter. "Nothing exists except matter." Then the atheistic convictions are matter, too. My opponents love atheism and hate religion. Are their love and hatred matter? They fight for an ideal, they write for an ideal, even while denying the existence of spiritual values. They themselves live on such values, even if they pervert them.

They write further: "The truth of dialectic materialism is confirmed by all the data of science and practice, whereas the justice of philosophic idealism and religion cannot be demonstrated by anybody."

So all the data of science and practice confirm that we are only matter! The authors of the book which I refute are also only matter! Does matter take the trouble to convince another quantity of matter? My opponents are a heap of matter; so am I. Why do they spend time and energy to change my opinions?

According to them, matter is in eternal movement, according to its own intrinsic laws. You cannot convince an atom to move other than its nature intends, as you cannot change the movements of a planet. Why do they then sit down to convince me?

Atheists are very often much better than their theories. Atheist soldiers died during the war to save the lives of their comrades. What idiot would die for the good of a wooden desk? Who would renounce any joy in order to make a piece of paper happy? Atheists, who give their lives for their comrades or who sacrifice their evenings to free others from religious superstition, do not themselves believe in the depths of their heart, that they and their comrades are only matter. Just as science cannot function without religion, so atheism and atheists cannot exist without respecting some of religion's basic values.

It is true that some scientists are in conflict with religion, but who knows how science will develop?

There is no reason to believe that the conflict even between certain scientists and religion is irreconcilable. And supposing it were, science and religion may seemingly disagree and yet both be true, as is the case with the two theories of light—one maintaining that light is a particle, the other that light is a wave. Both theories prove right in experiments. The idea that all truth must be synthesized in our mind is fallacious, since we are finite and can only know partial truths.

There is nothing threatening in the fact that two scientists, measuring accurately, arrive at different conclusions. Why then should it be distressing if a scientist on the one hand and a man of religion on the other hand, beginning with entirely different presuppositions, arrive at different results?

The case of Lord Rayleigh and Sir William Ramsay is known. They both found nitrogen by different methods, but there was always a slight difference between the atomic weights. They maintained their discordant results. They did not try to harmonize them; they saw no catastrophe in the disagreement. In the end, the conflict between the two results proved profitable for science. In the nitrogen of the one, Argon, an element unknown till then, was discovered.

We should not fear a conflict between religion and science as a whole. We have room in our hearts for all of reality. We would apply to this conflict the words of Jesus: "Let both grow together until the harvest" (Matthew 13:30). We would grant freedom to two conflicting opinions.

All this is hypothetical, because there must be something wrong with the discovery by my opponents of the terrible conflict between science and religion. Most scientists know nothing about the conflict.

With all due regard for the academic degrees of my adversaries, they will have to admit that Einstein knew at least a little bit more science than they. The proof is that our universe bears the name of Einstein and not the name of atheist authors. Einstein speaks about a higher intelligence which reveals itself through nature.

Perhaps you would like to know what the great physicist Max Planck says in his scientific autobiography. We quote his words:

Religion and natural science are fighting a joint battle in an incessant, never relaxing crusade against skepticism and against dogmatism, against disbelief and against superstition, and the rallying cry in this crusade has always been and always will be "Unto God."

The authors of *The Atheist's Handbook* are men of science. Then let them give a scientific explanation of the fact that such great scientists knew nothing about a conflict between science and religion! Max Planck even calls the contradiction between science and religion "a phantom problem."

The Atheist's Handbook makes this sweeping assertion: "Between science and religion there has always been an unceasing and implacable fight." They will never be able to substantiate this.

I quoted Einstein and Planck. What about other scientists? Did they know something about the conflict?

Sir Isaac Newton belongs to another century, but for all practical purposes we still live in the Newtonian universe. To mock his infidel friends, he made in his laboratory a solar system in miniature. An unbeliever asked him, "Who made it?" Newton answered, "Nobody." "Lies, stupidities!" the infidel answered. "Tell me the truth: who made it?" Then Newton replied, "It is nothing but a puny imitation of a much grander system, and I am not able to convince you that this mere toy is without a designer and maker! Did you profess to believe that the great original, from which the design is taken, has come into being without a maker? Tell me, by what sort of reasoning do you reach such an incongruous solution?"

The atheist professors acknowledge that Newton finishes his fundamental scientific work, *The Mathematical Principles of Natural Philosophy*, with words about "the ruling of a powerful and wise Being" and with expression of belief in an initial impulse, that is, a creation. They explain it by the fact that Newton lived in the beginning of the eighteenth century, when men were ignorant of many of the atomic and chemical and biological processes known today, when science was still tied up with theology. They also claim that the fact that Newton was religious was a hindrance to his science. But then remains the riddle that in the twentieth century the Newtonian universe has become the Einsteinian universe. Einstein knew at least something about the atomic processes, about the most recent developments of science, and he who had begun as an atheist in his youth was brought to faith by the fact that he arrived at the pinnacle of science.

My opponents mention with satisfaction Laplace, who said that he had no need of "the hypothesis" God. First of all, God has been vindicated by the fact that the great Soviet astronomer Tihov begins his book of astronomy with the assertion that we have no more need of the hypothesis Laplace. But all apart from this, Laplace was a professing Christian.

The authors of *The Atheist's Handbook* are wrong in quoting Descartes in support of their doctrines. Descartes was also a professing Christian. They distort the meaning of his words, giving them a materialistic sense. He wrote, "Give me matter and motion, and I will construct the universe!" The words are clear. The existence of the universe requires matter, motion, and an intelligent being to construct it. The words of Descartes are, "Give me matter and motion." Without this "me," matter and motion alone would not make a universe. It is only this "me," which comes from God, who can accomplish great deeds, because we have been created as creators.

One often wonders about the liberties academicians take in attributing to renowned authors ideas they never intended.

But let us leave these men of old and return to our own century.

Heisenberg, the great atomic scientist, could not have read *The Atheist's Handbook*, because he launched an appeal for a union between science and religion! Sir James Jeans, the renowned astronomer, writes in his book *The Mysterious Universe:*

> The universe begins to look more like a great thought than like a great machine. Mind no longer appears as an accidental intruder in the realm of matter. We are beginning to suspect, that we ought rather to hail it as the creator and governor of the realm of matter, not, of course, our individual minds, but the Mind in which the atoms out of which our individual minds have grown existed as thoughts...We discover that the universe shows evidence of a designing or controlling power, that has something in common with our individual minds. We are not so much strangers or intruders in the universe, as we first thought.

Newton had the disadvantage of belonging to a backward century. That is how *The Atheist's Handbook* explains his religiosity; it was only because of the pressure of his backward milieu that he wrote in his book *Optics*: "Does it not appear from phenomena that there is a Being, incorporeal, living, intelligent, omnipresent, with infinite space, which sees things intimately and thoroughly perceives them and comprehends them wholly by their immediate presence to himself?" But James Jeans belongs to our advanced scientific century, as does Heisenberg.

Let us listen to the great psychologist Professor Jung, who also belongs to our century:

> During the past thirty years, people from all civilized countries of the earth have consulted me… Among all my patients in their second half of life, that is to say over thirty-five years, there has not been one whose problem in the last resort was not that of finding a religious outlook on life. It is safe to say that everyone of them fell ill, because he had lost that which the living religions of every age have given to their followers, and none of them has been really healed who did not regain his religious outlook.

It is not the mentality of a century—it is science which makes men religious, science in all its spheres. Therefore, Kepler wrote centuries ago, "We are thinking God's thoughts after Him." And Sir Allister Hardy, formerly head of Oxford University's zoology department, wrote: "Some power we call God is involved in the process of life"; and "I believe the living world is as closely linked with theology as it is with physics and chemistry, that the divine element is part of the natural process, not strictly supernatural but paraphysical." He said something else that is very interesting: "Just as knowledge of the biology of sex does not destroy the lover, so a religion linked with science and natural theology need not destroy the rapture of communion with God. Let us go forward to reclaim the ground that has been lost in the world."

I do not know how it happened that *The Atheist's Handbook* refers to Bertrand Russell as a scientist. We know no scientific discovery of his. He is an authority for our opponents because he subscribed to leftist policies. But because his name has been mentioned, I think we should tell what he wrote about Christianity:

> There are certain things that our age needs, and certain things it should avoid. It needs compassion... It needs above all courageous hope and the impulse to create it... The root of the matter is a very simple and old-fashioned thing, a thing so simple that I am almost ashamed to mention it for fear of a derisive smile, with which wise cynics will greet my words. The thing I mean—please forgive me for mentioning it—is love. Christian love or compassion. If you feel this, you have a motive for existence, a guide for action, a reason for courage, an imperative necessity for an intellectual honesty.

Now let us come back to genuine scientists. C. Chant, professor of astrophysics at Toronto University, says, "I have no hesitation in asserting that at least ninety percent of astronomers have reached the conclusion that the universe is not the result of any blind law but is regulated by a great intelligence."

We repeat that if there is an irreconcilable conflict between science and religion, as atheists assert, most of the scientists themselves know nothing about it.

Atheists use as an anti-religious argument the science of cybernetics, by which they prove that all the workings of our mind are like the functioning of a machine; no spirit is implied in either.

It is truly marvelous that these cybernetics installations can reproduce or imitate nervous phenomena, that they translate, play chess, and solve problems of thought much more quickly than man can.

But—and this is the point so easily ignored—the cybernetics machine is produced by a mind. In the end, it is simply a reflection of the thought-processes of that mind and not something uniquely new.

Men can run, let us say, ten miles an hour. But they have invented jets and missiles which travel thousands of miles per hour. Men have eyes which perceive at a certain distance, but they have invented the microscope and the telescope to enable them to see what was hidden from the unaided eye. Men were created with the ability to make tools to extend their capabilities and enlarge their senses. The cybernetics machine belongs to this category, but behind every machine there is the mind which constructed it.

Who constructed the machine called "atheist author"? Let my opponents pause a bit and ponder the fact that every one of them has at his disposal around ten billion brain cells. What kind of Creator must He be who grants such a profusion of neurons to the one who wishes to mock Him! Any brain cell can be in contact with

25,000 others. The number of possible associations is of the order of ten billion to the twenty-five-thousandth power, a quantity larger than the probable number of atoms in the universe known to us.

Think further: each atheist has a thousand miles of blood vessels in his body to supply his brain and organs. To defeat old and proven religion is not an easy task; our opponents sweat at it. Each atheist author has one and a half million sweat glands on his body's surface. He breathes as he writes against religion. He can breathe because he has lungs composed of seven hundred million cells. While he writes against the Creator, his heart beats steadily; it beats many billions of times during his life. In fact, during an average lifetime it pumps the weight of some six hundred thousand tons of blood. Could my opponents believe that a crane which lifts such massive tonnage exists by itself without any involvement with an intelligent being?

Atheist authors have spent a tremendous amount of nervous energy on their writings. Now, the nervous system of every one of the authors has three trillion nerve cells, of which nine billion are in the cortex. Furthermore, they could not have written the book if they had not been healthy. Their health was ensured by the thirty million white corpuscles in their veins. They also have 130 quadrillion red corpuscles.

Doubtless they sometimes took a walk to stimulate their thinking before writing further. It rained; yet no drop of water fell into their nostrils, because the opening of the nostrils is downward, not upward. Who arranged for this small detail?

Oh, if these academicians only had the wisdom of the fisherman known as John the Evangelist! He wondered about the mystery of his heart, which was beating regularly, assuring the continuation of life. He lay down on the breast of his best friend, Jesus, heard the regular beatings of His heart, and so was reassured that there exists a God, just as the one who hears the regular ticking of a watch knows that there exists a watchmaker.

I hope with every fiber of my being that my opponents will also come to know this and to know it *now*—not in hell where the truth about God and His universe is finally realized, but too late!

From thinking about their own bodily machine, which is much more wonderful than the cybernetics one, let my opponents now turn to admire a long suspension bridge. Yet a spiderweb, strung across a garden path, suggested the first suspension bridge. But who gave the spider the intelligence which we admire in the engineer? And who provided it with a web of such remarkable tensile strength? Those who made the first airplanes, from Leonardo da Vinci to the Wright brothers, learned from the birds.

But my opponents may be sure that I understand them. They speak in the name of science, which is based on truth, and yet they themselves miss the one great condition of truth, which is free and fair discussion.

Suppose that several of the Communist academicians had arrived at religious conclusions, as Einstein and Planck have done. Could they have published a work expressing their convictions? Surely they could have—but only secretly and at the risk of going to prison. We cannot demand much from authors who write under such conditions. Not every man is a hero or a potential martyr.

The rulers of the Communist countries are more in love with their own doctrine than with objective truth and therefore do not submit it to the only valid test, that of free discussion; thus, they exclude their academicians from the right to speak in the name of science.

How can someone speak in the name of science when he attributes to religion what it has never asserted?

We will give below just a few examples, taken at random from *The Atheist's Handbook*. I quote: "According to the Bible, God has created all the stars, the sun, and the moon in the fourth day of creation." Here, my opponents have simply added the word "all." This one word does not exist in the respective verse of the Bible. The Bible teaches only this, that the stars were created by God; it does not exclude, as *The Atheist's Handbook* says, the appearance of new stars. God has created this universe according to laws established by Him, laws which allow for the possible appearance of new stars, as in other spheres there appear new men, new plans, and new ideas.

Another quotation from *The Atheist's Handbook:* "The preachers of religion declare that life has been created by God only on our planet, but science has demonstrated that life is very largely spread throughout the universe."

When did preachers of religion declare that life exists only on our planet? When did science demonstrate the second proposition?

Another quotation: "The transformation of nature by men shows obviously that the dogma, according to which the world created by God is invariable, has no foundation." Which religion ever asserted that the world created by God is invariable, or that men will not be able to transform nature? The Bible begins with the story that God put Adam in the garden of Eden to tend the garden, to work in it, which is to transform nature. Abel was a shepherd who bred animals, and Cain was a farmer. Men were meant to influence nature and to change it.

In the part of their book with the subtitle "The bankruptcy of the dogma of atonement," these atheists write: "Clergymen try to convince us that as God is omnipresent, the word of God has been incarnated simultaneously as at an order, and in every one of the worlds inhabited by living beings. So Christ had to be born, to suffer and to die simultaneously on an infinite number of planets." I defy my opponents to give the name of one single clergyman who has ever endorsed such foolishness. First of all, science has never established that there exist intelligent beings on other planets; secondly, no clergyman has ever said that Christ died on many planets.

But we do not need to insist on this, because a few pages later the atheist authors say just the opposite of what they invented before. Now, they put in the mouth of theologians (nobody knows which) the assertion that the earth is the only place in which mankind has committed sin, which required atonement, whereas other races on other planets have remained faithful. Invention after invention! Never have theologians dogmatized about these questions!

With a smile, I give another quotation from *The Atheist's Handbook:* "Religion admits only the natural modification of the geography of our planet, because it comes from God, but the creative intervention of man in the geographic process is completely excluded." They mean by this that religion does not allow the creation of canals for irrigation. That the very religious people of old had a vast network of irrigation canals does not count for them. When has religion pronounced itself against canals? What religion?

Well, this time my opponents have proof. They quote prince Golitsin, governor of the province of Astrakhan of some two hundred years ago, who opposed a canal uniting two rivers. But I for one have never known governors of a province to be representatives of religion.

Another quotation: "The clergymen have preached for thousands of years the idea that the flying of men towards heaven without the permission of God is inadmissible, profane, and have persecuted with cruelty and have exterminated the courageous men who have tried to fulfill such flights, not to speak about the cosmic travels of men; and in the present, all these religious principles have been destroyed."

I try to be polite, but I cannot say otherwise than that this is a patent lie. Nobody can give the name of one single man who has tried to fly and who has been exterminated because of this. Are astronauts exterminated in America? The first American astronaut asserted his faith in God, and the astronauts that followed read the Bible while in orbit around the moon. They came back, they were feasted. Not one of them was killed. How can academicians write such lies?

I continue with these curious quotations from the atheists' book: "Some preachers of religion say that the Most High has moved His inhabitants in the depths of the universe and that therefore the cosmic rockets and satellites do not reach as far as the kingdom of heaven. Why did God need to move into another apartment?" When did any preacher of religion ever propound such stupidity?

But the atheist authors very soon forget what they have said and fight against us with another argument: "The clergymen underline especially that men cannot find God or His supernatural servants, because these are immaterial, without a body, and belong to the spiritual world, not to the material world." This already sounds better, but they do not accept the fact that God, being spirit, is not meant to be seen by an astronaut who has gone only as far as the moon. They write: "The immaterial is also accessible to man." Poor materialists, who said only a few pages earlier that nothing exists except matter and movement! Now they acknowledge that the immaterial exists and is accessible to the human mind—which is true, if only they would use their minds to discover the Eternal Spirit and their own spirit.

Another gratuitous assertion of *The Atheist's Handbook* is that religion justifies ignorance. Who created the first universities in Europe? Was it not the Christians? Were not the monasteries the first centers of culture? Who would deny that the German and English languages—and many others—were formed by the Bible?

I think that the quotations given above are sufficient. They will make some readers so disgusted that they will ask themselves if it is worthwhile to answer a book written on such a low level. But it has to be answered, because the book is distributed by the millions in innumerable translations. It is inculcated in the minds of youth; it dominates by the power of the whip.

No, science cannot be opposed to religion. Science can be opposed only to a certain kind of backward religion.

If I pronounce the word "ship," this can awaken in your mind different images. You can have before you the ark of Noah, the primitive ship on which the Polynesians traversed the oceans, the ships of the Vikings when they first arrived in America, a steamer of a hundred years ago, or a modem trans-Atlantic luxury liner.

When I say "religion" or "God," again this awakens in the mind different images. Different men at different times, according to their powers of understanding, feeling, and spiritual insight, have understood God differently. They interpreted His revelation differently also.

Some concepts of God are backward and undoubtedly contradict science. But this does not apply to all religion; nor does religion have to accept all science, because there exist many backward things in science too.

Science and religion belong to two different spheres. Science tells us only what the material aspects of things are. If a scientist were asked what a kiss is, he would say, "It is the approaching of two pairs of lips with a reciprocal transmission of microbes and carbon dioxide." But there is a "more" to the kiss. From the scientific point of view, any flower is the balance of a biochemical mechanism requiring potash, phosphates, nitrogen, and water in definite proportions; but every lover of flowers will contest that the scientist has said everything about a flower. Science goes only halfway. Part of the way is gone by art, part by philosophy, and the last mile by religion.

You know very little about life if you think of it only as a protoplasmic organism, forgetting what you have learned about it from Shakespeare, from Dickens, from Michelangelo, from Raphael, from the great religious personalities of the world, and from the incarnation of God, Jesus Christ.

Would it be right to speak of a lover's embrace in terms of an accelerated release of adrenaline into the blood and say that this is an adequate explanation of everything that happens at that moment?

It is unscientific and therefore untrue to reduce life to science.

The authors of *The Atheist's Handbook* pass from theoretical considerations about the relationship between science and religion to the practical side of things. Luther allegedly asked for "fierce repressions against the heresy of Copernicus." It remains a mystery when Luther ever asked for these repressions. You would seek in vain for any such words in the works of Luther.

"But did Calvin not burn Servetus, the great scientist?" our opponents ask. Yes, he had him burned, unhappily. But the assertion of *The Atheist's Handbook* that Calvin burned him at the stake for his scientific discoveries is simply not true. He was sentenced to death for teaching a false religious doctrine. This was some five hundred years ago and it is very regrettable, but it is not for our opponents to say a word about this. Not one Servetus, but tens of millions of men have been sentenced to death or killed slowly in Communist concentration camps for having dared to nurture a political doctrine other than that of a dictator later disowned by his own comrades.

Neither is another assertion of my opponents true, that the library of Alexandria was destroyed by Christian fanatics at the end of the fourth century. If they had done so, the Muslims would not have been able to destroy it, as they did in the seventh century.

Neither what the authors of *The Atheist's Handbook* say theoretically about science and religion, nor what they say on the practical side of the matter, can stand investigation.

It is now an axiom of biology that function creates the organ. We have eyes to see light and color. We have ears because there are sounds for us to hear, and hands because there are material things to handle. We are given a brain because there are things to think about. How is it that we have the curious capacity to believe, to have faith? Even a child has this capacity. So there must be a corresponding reality. Would it be logical in this world, where everything in us corresponds to an external reality, for just this capacity of faith to be in us without something "out there" to be apprehended by faith? We have the capacity for belief because there is a God to believe in. There exists not only matter, but also a reality which cannot be explained in physical or chemical terms without exposing oneself to ridicule.

Science pleads for religion.

The earth is exactly at the right distance from the sun and has the right orbital velocity to make life possible on it. If we had been a little bit nearer the sun, we would have been burned by its fire. If we had been farther away, the earth would have been too cold for anything to grow. If the earth did not revolve around the sun, there would not be seasonal changes.

Proteins are a combination of five major elements: carbon, hydrogen, nitrogen, sulphur, and oxygen. Within every molecule of protein, there are probably something like forty to fifty thousand atoms. From roughly a hundred chemical elements which are distributed at random on our earth, only these five, and then only in fixed proportions, can form molecules of protein. Could this have happened by chance? The quantity of matter that would have had to be shaken up and the length of time required to finish this task in order to obtain proteins by chance, can be calculated according to the laws of probability. The Swiss mathematician Charles Cuye has made this calculation. He says: "The probability against such an occurrence by chance is 1:10 with 160 zeros following." It means that there is one chance in 10^{160} that out of a random shaking together of matter, one single molecule of protein would be produced. The matter to be shaken would have to be greater than that of the whole known universe. The time needed for this would be 10^{243} billions of years!

Professor J. Leathes has calculated that the links of a chain in a very simple protein are combined in 10^{160} millions of ways. Chance cannot build such a molecule. Chance has never built the frame of a house or a piano, which are both very simple things compared to one molecule of protein.

When I was in prison, I heard quarrels between thieves. They played with dice. If a die happened to turn up a six too often, the other thieves immediately suspected that the dice were loaded and that chance was not operating. It could not just happen that sixes should turn up again and again. Neither could simple chance have given us the ordered universe that we have. A philosopher, even an atheist philosopher, cannot be the result of the development of matter at random. Simple chance would never result in an atheist thinker.

I quoted a mathematician to the effect that the chance for creating one protein molecule would be 1 to 10^{160}. Would any of my atheist opponents put a penny in a lottery in which the chance for gain would be 1 to 10^{160}? It would be a stupid risk. It would mean throwing a penny away. But they risk their mental sanity, they risk the eternal jewel of their soul, they risk the truth on a theory that has as many chances to be exact as the chance to win in our hypothetical lottery. Professor Edwyn Conklin, a well-known biologist at Princeton University, has said, "The probability of life originating from an accident is comparable to the probability of the unabridged dictionary resulting from an explosion in a print-ing shop."

But all our arguments are of no avail for confirmed atheists. They know about the skull of the Neanderthal and others like him to prove that Adam, who lived in Paradise in fellowship with God, could not have existed. The Bible begins with something unscientific; our predecessors were very primitive men, evolved from the animal world, they say. There can be no question of any concordance between the Bible and science.

Suppose that excavations will be made on earth 5,000 years from now and archaeologists will find two or three skulls of Australian aborigines, or of men still living in the stone age in New Guinea. The anthropologists of that day will say that in our time, there lived no civilized men. But men who launch rockets to the moon coexist with the pygmies. Why should not some of Adam's mentally developed descendants have coexisted with cave men?

I think I have said enough about this subject of science and religion.

What keeps these atheistic authors from claiming the right to speak in the name of truth is the complete lack of doubt in their book.

The authors of the Bible, though deeply religious people, never abstained from expressing their doubts. You find them in the Psalms and in the Book of Job. Even John the Baptist had doubts when in prison about Jesus being the Messiah. Jesus Himself cried on the cross, "My God, my God, why have you forsaken me?" (Matthew 27:46).

No man is entirely religious. Religious men have their doubts. Likewise no man is always an atheist. Atheists have their moments of faith, but whereas authors of the Bible—David and Job, for example—sometimes have thoughts that almost seem blasphemous, our atheist opponents are always very predictable. They are all of a piece: atheists, and only atheists! This is not natural. They do not express all that they think.

It is as if they had never even heard about Heisenberg's famous uncertainty principle!

Scientific truth is on our side. Jesus can be considered the founder of scientific thought. He said, "Go and tell John what you hear and see" (Matthew 11:4); "We speak of what we know, and bear witness to what we have seen" (John 3:11); and "Look at the birds of the air... consider the lilies of the field, how they grow" (Matthew 6:26,28). He teaches exact observation! Christians are taught to speak what they know, what they have heard and seen. Science is based on these same principles.

31

ATONEMENT

I owe my opponents something. Christ taught us to reward evil with good. They have slandered our religion; I must show them the way of salvation. Authors of an atheistic book of propaganda can be saved just as surely as those who have committed other sins.

We live with this terrible reality of sin. I have my sins; atheists have theirs. Neither humanistic nor atheistic nor religious philosophy, nor speculations of clergymen or of their godless foes can do anything toward freeing a man from his sin. For this, God has done a mighty, efficacious work. I have sought to prove the reliability of Scriptures. Atheists can learn from Scripture how to be cleansed from their sins, to become children of God and heirs of eternal life.

Paul writes: "Christ died for our sins in accordance with the Scriptures,...he was buried,...he was raised on the third day in accordance with the Scriptures" (1 Corinthians 15:3,4).

Nobody can understand fully what the death of Christ in Palestine two thousand years ago has to do with *my* sins, and how *my* sins can be removed by a sacrifice which *He* made at that time.

But neither can we give a full explanation of the nature of electricity, or of gravity, or of our own physiological and psychological processes. We do not need a full explanation of the atonement in order to profit from it. It is enough to believe that Christ died for our sins, that He bore our punishment, and that our sins are no more imputed to us.

Christ is God incarnate. Yet He humbled Himself and took upon Himself the penalty of our sins in His own suffering. Peter puts it in these words: "You were ransomed from the futile ways inherited from your forefathers, not with perishable things such as silver or gold, but with the precious blood of Christ, like that of a lamb without blemish or spot" (1 Peter 1:18,19). And in heaven a song is sung to the praise of Christ: "You were slain, and by your blood you ransomed people for God from every tribe and language and people and nation, and you have made them a kingdom and priests to our God, and they shall reign on the earth" (Revelation 5:9,10).

When Christ purchased by His blood men of every nation, He purchased also the Communists and the atheists.

As I have said: We cannot fully understand the atonement, but we can understand something of it. When we bear in mind that Christ is God and, as such, a person of infinite value and dignity, then (I know the assertion will shock, but still I do not hesitate to make it) the killing of Christ was a worse crime than that which would have been committed if the entire human race had been crucified. You will understand this better if you will meditate on the words of Isaiah: "The nations are like a drop from a bucket, and are accounted as the dust on the scales" before God (Isaiah 40:15).

A very simple illustration will show what we think. I am sick with tuberculosis, and I have killed millions of tuberculin microbes with medicines. I have also killed many other microbes and all kinds of insects. Many animals have been killed for my food; I suffer no remorse for these. But my conscience accuses me of every wrong I have done to man, because man is so much higher than the insects—he bears the image of God. In the same way, Christ, who is God incarnate, is of infinitely higher value than the billions of beings who are only men, and therefore His crucifixion was fully sufficient to redeem the whole human race from all its sins—this on condition of faith in what He has done for us. In His person, God suffered and died for His people, appropriating to Himself first a human body in which He should be able to die, because the Godhead is immortal.

Therefore, Peter writes again, "Christ also suffered once for sins, the righteous for the unrighteous, that he might bring us to God" (1 Peter 3:18). And John writes, "The blood of Jesus his Son cleanses us from all sin" (1 John 1:7). John the Baptist said, pointing to Jesus, "Behold, the Lamb of God, who takes away the sin of the world!" (John 1:29). Paul writes, "Since, therefore, we have now been justified by his blood, much more shall we be saved by him from the wrath of God" (Romans 5:9). What wrath such a blasphemous work as *The Atheist's Handbook* must have provoked in God! But we can be saved from this wrath, because "in [Jesus

Christ] we have redemption through his blood, the forgiveness of our trespasses, according to the riches of his grace" (Ephesians 1:7).

The atonement has been the object of meditation on the part of Christians for two thousand years. It has been explained in diverse manners. There are many doctrines of the atonement.

Which of them should we choose?

Therese of Lisieux, when asked which Christian virtue she would like to practice most, answered, "All of them!" I would say the same thing about the doctrines of the atonement. They are all the result of deep meditation of believing and loving souls; there is no reason to put any of them aside.

True is the vicarious doctrine, that Jesus died as our substitute for our sins. True also is the moral influence doctrine, that Christ died in order that through the beauty of His gesture and of His sacrifice, He might influence us to adopt a new and godly manner of life. True is the governmental theory, according to which God freely forgives sinners but made Christ suffer in order to show us that every transgression incurs punishment, and that we, looking at the great suffering of Christ, might see what we deserved for our sins. True is the mystical theory, according to which Christ and the believing soul are one, united by a love which makes them indissoluble. As a mother suffers with her sick child and as a loving bride suffers with her bridegroom who passes through pain, we have suffered together with our beloved Christ on Golgotha, and we ourselves have received in His body, with which we are one, punishment for our sins.

But I think that the most plausible explanation for a twentieth century man is the doctrine of transfer. We all have in our psychology the mechanism of transfer. When we cannot find something and we are upset about it, it is enough for us to blame someone else—our wife or our child—for misplacing the respective object. We have found a scapegoat on whom to place the guilt. If a child has banged himself against a stool, it is enough for the mother to "spank" the stool for the hurt it caused, and the child is immediately mollified. The mechanism of transfer is deeply rooted in us. Our heart finds peace if we can charge somebody else with our troubles: the monarchy, the landlords, the Americans, the imperialists, the Jews, the blacks, the whites, anybody but ourself.

Jesus consciously used this mechanism of transfer; therefore He came to mankind, presenting Himself as the Son of God. It was as if He said: "Now, if you have this tendency to transfer your sins to somebody else, the most normal thing is to transfer them to My shoulders. I bear the responsibility, because the whole creation was made through Me. I am ready to take upon Myself all the guilt and all the sin. You feel that your sins deserve a punishment. Kant said, 'The criminal has a right to punishment.' I will bear the punishment which you deserve, and you will be free."

I recommend to my atheist opponents, since they have done harm to so many millions of souls by writing slanderous lies against religion, that they put this crime on the shoulders of Christ, whom they have attacked. Christ is the Lamb of God who takes away the sin of the whole world; therefore, He takes away also the sins of the atheists. Believe in Christ, and you will be saved!

You have tried to oppose religion with atheistic theories. This is childish. Critical analysis is impotent before interior anguish. Atheistic theories do not help a dying man or his bereaved family. Your own doctrines are of no value to you when you pass through the anguish of doubt and ask yourself if you have not committed a terrible offense. You may not think about it today, but there will come a day when you will have to think, the day of your death.

Major cities around the world are competing to see which will be the city of greatest influence. None of them will! The city with the mightiest population, the city where kings and commoners, capitalists and Communists, atheists and religious people, clergymen and their enemies meet, is the city of the grave. And for the unbeliever, beyond the grave lies only remorse.

Even at the moment before death, it will not be too late. In that moment, you can pray, "Lord Jesus, Son of God, pity me, the sinner!" Believe in the blood shed for you by Jesus Christ, and you will be saved.

My dear atheist friends, we have passed a few hours together. Now we part.

In the Bible the story is recounted that while the Jews were slaves in Egypt, for three days there was a spell of darkness. While the darkness surrounding the Egyptians was so dense that they could not see one another, all the children of Israel enjoyed light.

This light is the Word of God. The people of God had this light, and it shone into their hearts.

It is told that when Palestine was under Turkish rule, a cruel official forbade the Jews to kindle lights at night. The cities were completely shrouded in darkness.

But in Safed, the windows of the rabbi Joseph Caro glowed at night. The rabbi read the Scriptures. The guards reported to the official what was happening. He immediately rode to the rabbi's house and saw him leaning over the Bible, while the entire room was aglow with a luminescence coming from the walls, although no lamp was burning in the room. The walls were covered with fireflies. They gave him light.

The rabbi explained to the official, "The law of God illuminates not only the lives of those who study it, but also the fireflies who listen."

Some of you, my atheistic opponents, and those who have believed you will read these lines. I am sure that they will be illumined, though their minds have been darkened by your slanders against the Word of God, and that bright light, the light of Christ, will shed its warmth and beauty throughout all lands.

32

A LAST WORD

Seven hundred pages of denial after denial—denial of God, the Bible, eternal life, and humanity—shows an excess of zeal with the authors of *The Atheist's Handbook*.

You atheists write boring books. It is not your fault. You cannot do better. Every man has a God-shaped vacuum in his heart. Instead of filling the vacuum with God, you write books about the structure and beauties of a vacuum.

You are compelled to write them. Atheist books are the only books about atheism, whereas Luther said, "Our Lord has written the promise of the resurrection not in books alone, but in every leaf of springtime."

Your books are boring, yes. But they are also poisonous for minds which don't have the liberty to read religious books and thus come to a knowledge of the truth. You are like someone who leads caterpillars astray by telling them that all their endeavors are in vain; they will never become beautiful butterflies. You tell buds that they will never become flowers. You kill the souls of men, telling them that they are not destined to be Christlike in this life and in Paradise for all eternity.

I don't wish to insult you. I wish to help you realize your terribly dangerous state of heart. You are worse than murderers. They kill only bodies. You slay souls, incapacitating them for enjoying God.

Therefore I give you the advice which Sonya gave to the murderer Raskolnikov: "Get up. Go at once, this very minute, and stand at the crossroads; then bow down and kiss first the earth which you have defiled, and then bow to the world, to all four points of the compass, and say to them all aloud, 'I have killed.' Then God will send you life again. Will you go? Will you go?"

I myself bow before you, because I also have killed souls in the past.

Like you, I was an atheist, until the day I came to myself and did literally what Sonya advised. Now I shudder at the life of violence and suffering that awaits you if you continue in your atheism. I have been found by Christ and have been saved from atheism, from crime. This way is open for you, too.

Will you go? Will you go?

ABOUT THE VOICE
OF THE MARTYRS

The Voice of the Martyrs (VOM) is a nonprofit, interdenominational Christian organization dedicated to serving persecuted Christians on the world's most difficult and dangerous mission fields and bringing other members of the body of Christ into fellowship with them. VOM was founded in 1967 by Pastor Richard Wurmbrand and his wife, Sabina. Richard was imprisoned 14 years in Communist Romania for his faith in Christ, and Sabina was imprisoned for three years. They were ransomed out of Romania in 1965 and soon established a global network of missions dedicated to assisting persecuted Christians.

To be inspired by the courageous faith of our persecuted brothers and sisters in Christ who are advancing the gospel in hostile areas and restricted nations, request a free subscription to VOM's award-winning monthly magazine. Visit us at vom.org, or call 800-747-0085.

To learn more about VOM's work, please contact us:

United States	vom.org
Australia	vom.com.au
Belgium	hvk-aem.be
Brazil	maisnomundo.org
Canada	vomcanada.com
Czech Republic	hlas-mucedniku.cz
Finland	marttyyrienaani.fi
Germany	verfolgte-christen.org
The Netherlands	sdok.nl
New Zealand	vom.org.nz
Poland	gpch.pl
Portugal	vozdosmartires.com
Singapore	gosheninternational.org
South Africa	persecutionsa.org
South Korea	vomkorea.kr
United Kingdom	releaseinternational.org

ABOUT THE AUTHOR

Pastor Richard Wurmbrand (1909–2001) was an evangelical minister who endured a total of fourteen years of Communist imprisonment and torture in his homeland of Romania. Few names are better known in Romania, where he is one of the most widely recognized Christian leaders, authors, and educators.

In 1945, when the Communists seized Romania and attempted to control the churches for their purposes, Richard Wurmbrand immediately began an effective, vigorous "underground" ministry to his enslaved people as well as the invading Russian soldiers. He was arrested in 1948. His wife was later arrested and sentenced to prison and slave labor for three years on the Danube Canal. Richard Wurmbrand spent three years in solitary confinement, seeing no one but his Communist torturers. He was then transferred to a group cell, where the torture continued for five more years.

Due to his international stature as a Christian leader, diplomats of foreign embassies asked the Communist government about his safety and were informed that he had fled Romania. Secret police, posing as released fellow-prisoners, told his wife of attending his burial in the prison cemetery. His family in Romania and his friends abroad were told to forget him because he was dead.

After eight and a half years in prison, he was released and immediately resumed his work with the underground church. A couple of years later, in 1959, he was re-arrested and sentenced to twenty-five years in prison.

Pastor Wurmbrand was released in a general amnesty in 1964, and again continued his underground ministry. Realizing the great danger of a third imprisonment, Christians in Norway negotiated with the Communist authorities for his release from Romania. The Communist government had begun "selling" their political prisoners. The "going price" for a prisoner was $1,900; the price for Wurmbrand was $10,000.

In May 1966, he testified before the US Senate's Internal Security Subcommittee and stripped to the waist to show the scars of eighteen deep torture wounds covering his torso. His story was carried across the world in newspapers throughout the US, Europe, and Asia. Wurmbrand was warned in September 1966 that the Communist regime of Romania planned to assassinate him; yet he was not silent in the face of this death threat.

Founders of the Christian mission The Voice of the Martyrs, he and his wife traveled throughout the world inspiring the establishment of a network of offices that provide relief to the families of imprisoned Christians in Islamic nations, Communist Vietnam, China, and other countries where Christians are persecuted for their faith. His message has been, "Hate the evil systems, but love your persecutors. Love their souls, and try to win them for Christ."

Pastor Wurmbrand authored numerous books, which have been translated into numerous languages and distributed globally.

OTHER BOOKS BY
RICHARD WURMBRAND

Tortured for Christ

Karl Marx and the Satanic Roots of Communism

If Prison Walls Could Speak

The Oracles of God

In God's Underground

100 Prison Meditations

Christ on the Jewish Road

The Overcomers

Victorious Faith

Reaching Toward the Heights

Alone With God

Proofs of God's Existence

With God in Solitary Confinement

From the Lips of Children

The Midnight Bride

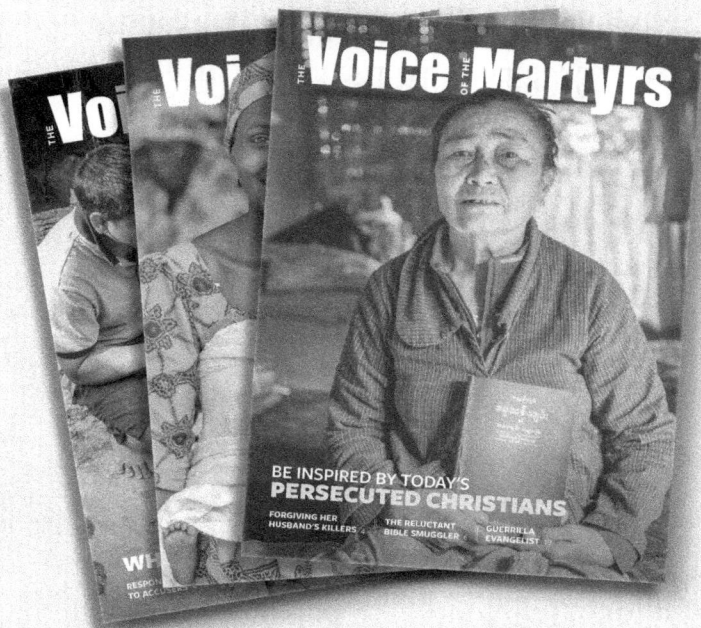

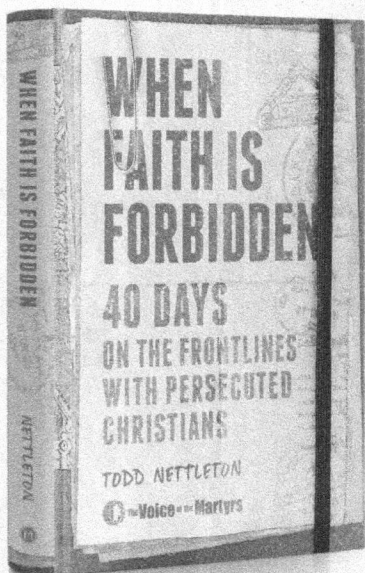

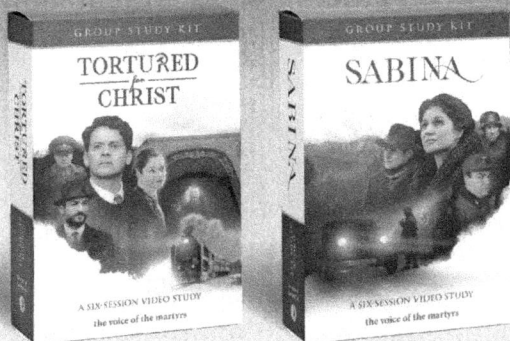

The Voice of the Martyrs

INSPIRE KIDS AND TEENS

WITNESSES TRILOGY BOXED SET

These three animated films take you from Christ's birth through the birth of the early church. Inspire children and young adults with the retelling of Christ's life and sacrificial death, and watch as His followers take His message to the ends of the earth.

THE TORCHLIGHTERS ULTIMATE ACTIVITY BOOK AND DVD SET

The Voice of the Martyrs presents a 144-page, full-color activity book to complement the award-winning Torchlighters DVD series.

VOM GRAPHIC NOVEL

This full-color, graphic novel anthology covers the earliest period of church history — from A.D. 34 to A.D. 203 — including the time of the apostles and early church martyrs.

COURAGEOUS SERIES

Inspire your children with the true stories of biblical heroes and saints. VOM's Courageous Series books highlight the lives of faithful Christians from history, showing how they boldly proclaimed Christ in the face of persecution. Includes the stories of Stephen, Thomas, the Apostle Paul, Nicholas, Patrick and Valentine.

FREE RESOURCES

CHOOSE ONE OF THESE RESOURCES FOR FREE AT **VOM.ORG/KIDS-FREE**

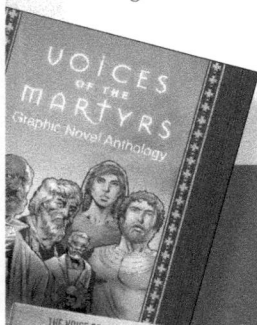

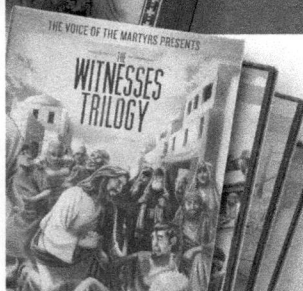